WASTE MANAGEMENT AND ENVIRONMENTAL HEALTH

ENV BOOKS SERIES

WASTE MANAGEMENT AND ENVIRONMENTAL HEALTH

Editors

Dr. B. Tabassum
Assistant Professor
Department of Zoology
Govt. Raza P.G. College
Rampur - 244 901 (U.P.)
(India)
Email: *dr.btabassum@gmail.com*

Dr. Priya Bajaj
Assistant Professor
Department of Zoology
Govt. Raza P.G. College
Rampur - 244 901 (U.P.)
(India)
Email: *drpriyabajaj73@gmail.com*

Dr. Pawan Kumar 'Bharti'
Vice President
Society for Environment, Health, Awareness of Nutrition & Toxicology (SEHAT)
1775, Sohan Ganj, Near Clock Tower
Delhi - 110 007 (India)
E-mail: *gurupawanbharti@rediffmail.com*

Associate Editors

Dr. Virendra Kumar
Plant Protection Officer
Kanpur (U.P.)
(India)

Ms. Alina Javed
Jamia Millia Islamia
New Delhi
(India)

DISCOVERY PUBLISHING HOUSE PVT. LTD.
NEW DELHI-110 002

Published by:

Namit Wasan

DISCOVERY PUBLISHING HOUSE PVT. LTD.

4383/4B, Ansari Road, Darya Ganj

New Delhi-110 002 (India)

Phone : +91-11-23279245, 43596064-65

Fax : +91-11-23253475

E-mail : discoverypublishinghouse@gmail.com

namitwasan9@gmail.com

sales@discoverypublishinggroup.com

web : www.discoverypublishinggroup.com

***First Edition:* 2016**

ISBN: 978-93-5056-777-7

Waste Management and Environmental Health

Printed at:

Infinity Imaging Systems

Delhi

ENV Books Series, India

Calls lengthy and error free chapters for further volumes of books on various environmental issues. (Send your manuscripts to envbooks@gmail.com)

***Founding Editor* (*Editor-in-Chief*)**

Dr. Pawan Kumar 'Bharti'
Society for Environment, Health, Awareness of Nutrition & Toxicology (SEHAT-India)
1775, Sohanganj, Near Clock Tower, Delhi-7, (India)
E-mail:*gurupawanbharti@rediffmail.com*

Other Titles by Editor-in-Chief:

1. **Advances in Biotechnology and Ecological Sciences (2013)**
   Bharti, P.K., Chauhan, A. and Ray, J. (eds.)
   (ISBN: 978-93-5056-358-8).
2. **Advances in Agriculture and Ecology (2013)**
   Bharti, P.K.; Chauhan, A. and Ezeaku Peter Ikemefuna (eds.)
   (ISBN: 978-93-5056-362-5).
3. **Agriculture and Environmental Biotechnology (2014)**
   Bharti, P.K. and Chauhan, A. (eds.)
   (ISBN: 978-93-5056-479-0).
4. **Agriculture Development and Sustainable Environment (2015)**
   Ray, J. and Bharti, P. K. (eds.)
   (ISBN: 978-93-5056-759-3)
5. **Agriculture Ecology and Environment (2014)**
   Bharti, P.K. and Olubukola O. Babalola (eds.)
   (ISBN: 978-93-5056-480-6).
6. **Agriculture, Environment and Nano-science (2015)**
   Bharti, Pawan K. (ed.)
   (ISBN: 978-93-5056-760-5)

7. **Agro-biodiversity Conservation & Sustainable Development (2016)**
Sharma, Pankaj; Singh, Narayan; and Bharti, P.K. (eds.)
(ISBN: 978-93-505-782-1)

8. **Agro-forestry and Climate Change (2014)**
Bharti, Pawan K. and Singh, Narayan (eds.)
(ISBN: 978-93-5056-514-8).

9. **Aquaculture and Fisheries Environment (2014)**
Gupta, S.K. and Pawan K. Bharti (eds.)
(ISBN: 978-93-5056-408-0).

10. **Aquatic Biodiversity and Pollution (2013)**
Bharti, P.K.; Chauhan, A. and Kaoud, H.A.H. (eds.)
(ISBN: 978-93-5056-359-5).

11. **Aquatic Ecology and Biotechnology (2014)**
Bharti, P.K. and Zaki, M.S.A. (eds.)
(ISBN: 978-93-5056-451-6).

12. **Aquatic Environment and Toxicology (2013)**
Bharti, Pawan K. (ed.)
(ISBN: 978-93-5056-236-9).

13. **Biodiversity, Biotechnology and Environmental Conservation (2015)**
Bharti, P.K. and Bhandari, G. (eds.)
(ISBN: 978-93-5056-750-0).

14. **Biodiversity of Aquatic Ecosystem: *Significance, Threat and Conservation* (2013)**
Bharti, P.K. and Kaoud, H.A.H. (eds.)
(ISBN: 978-93-5056-297-0).

15. **Bioremediation and Microbial Biotechnology (2016)**
Gupta, Sandeep; and Bharti, P.K. (eds.)
(ISBN: 978-93-5056-783-8)

16. **Biotechnological Approaches & Water Ecosystem (2016)**
Zaki, M.S.A.; and Bharti, P.K. (eds.)
(ISBN: 978-93-5056-779-1)

17. **Biotechnology, Agro-ecology and Environment (2015)**
Chauhan, Avnish and Bharti, P.K. (eds.)
(ISBN: 978-93-5056-757-9).

18. **Clean Technologies and Environmental Protection (2015)**
Chauhan, A.; Sharma, S. and Bharti, P.K. (eds.)
(ISBN: 978-93-5056-731-9).

19. **Climate Change and Agriculture (2012)**
Bharti, P.K. and Chauhan, Avnish (eds.)
(ISBN: 978-93-5056-148-5).

20. **Climate Change and Biodiversity (2013)**
Bharti, P.K. and Chauhan, Avnish (eds.)
(ISBN: 978-93-5056-360-1).

21. **Conservation and Cultivation of Medicinal Plants (2015)**
Bharti, P.K. and Singh Narayan (eds.)
(ISBN: 978-93-5056-740-1).

22. **Eco-toxicology and Eco-technology (2013)**
Bharti, P.K. and Zaki, M. (eds.)
(ISBN: 978-93-5056-313-7).

23. **Environmental Biotechnology and Application (2013)**
Bharti, P.K. and Chauhan, Avnish (eds.)
(ISBN: 978-93-5056-262-8).

24. **Environmental Conservation and Biotechnology (2014)**
Chauhan, A. and P.K. Bharti (eds.)
(ISBN: 978-93-5056-512-4).

25. **Environmental Health and Problems (2013)**
Bharti, P.K. and Gajananda, Kh. (eds.)
(ISBN: 978-93-5056-263-5).

26. **Environmental Pollution and Biodiversity (2012)**
Bharti, P.K.; Chauhan, Avnish and Kumar, P. (eds.)
(ISBN: 978-93-5056-149-2).

27. **Fisheries and Toxicology (2014)**
Zaki, M.S.A.; Bharti, P.K. and Chauhan, A. (eds.)
(ISBN: 978-93-5056-452-3).

28. **Fish Habitat and Aquaculture (2015)**
Bharti, P.K.; Gupta Kr. Sanjay (eds.)
(ISBN: 978-93-5056-744-9).

29. **Freshwater Ecosystem and Xenobiotics (2013)**
Bharti, P.K.; Zaki, M. and Chauhan, A. (eds.)
(ISBN: 978-93-5056-299-4).

30. **Limnology and Aquatic Science (2015)**
Sharma, S. and Bharti, P.K. (eds.)
(ISBN: 978-93-5056-735-7).

31. **Medicinal Plants: *Distribution, Utilization and Significance* (2015)**
Sharma, P.; Bharti, P.K. and Narayan Singh (eds.)
(ISBN: 978-93-5056-734-0).

32. **Microbial Applications and Environment (2014)**
Bharti, Pawan K. (ed.)
(ISBN: 978-93-5056-515-5).

33. **Microbial Ecology and Habitat (2014)**
Bharti, Pawan K. (ed.)
(ISBN: 978-93-5056-514-8).

34. **Natural Ecosystem and Climate Change (2015)**
Bharti, P.K., and Kh. Gajananda (ed.)
(ISBN: 978-93-5056-745-6).

35. **Prakriti me Aushadhi (*in Hindi*) (2012)**
Singh, J.R.; Bharti, P.K. and Bharti, B.
(ISBN: 978-93-5056-200-0).

36. **Seed Technology, Plant Growth and Cropping System (2015)**
Tyagi, P.K. and Bharti, P.K. (eds.)
(ISBN: 978-93-5056-738-8).

37. **Soil Characteristics and Agro-ecology (2015)**
Avnish Chauhan and Bharti, P.K. (eds.)
(ISBN: 978-93-5056-758-6).

38. **Soil Contamination and Conservation (2015)**
Ezeaku, P.I. and Bharti, P.K. (eds.)
(ISBN: 978-93-5056-737-1).

39. **Soil Quality and Contamination (2013)**
Bharti, P.K. and Chauhan, Avnish (eds.)
(ISBN: 978-93-5056-361-8).

40. **Waste Disposal and Management (2015)**
Bharti, P.K.; Tabassum, B. and Bajaj, P. (eds.)
(ISBN: 978-93-5056-729-6).

41. **Water Resources and Agriculture (2014)**
Bharti, P.K. and Ezeaku Peter Ikemefuna (eds.)
(ISBN: 978-93-5056-481-3).

Preface

"Human society sustains itself by transforming nature into Waste"

Throughout most of history, the amount of waste generated by humans was insignificant due to low population density and low societal levels of the exploitation of natural resources. Common waste produced during pre-modern times was mainly ashes and human-biodegradable waste, and these were released back into the ground locally, with minimum environmental impact. Tools made out of wood or metal were generally reused or passed down through the generations. Following the onset of industrialization and the sustained urban growth of large population centers, the buildup of waste in the cities caused a rapid deterioration in levels of sanitation and the general quality of urban life. The streets became choked with filth due to the lack of waste clearance regulations.

The stench and ugly sight of garbage dumped on the roadside, sometimes overflowing from drains or floating on the surface of rivers, is not at all uncommon in India. It is disgusting, until you get used to it and begin to ignore it. India's waste generation stands at 0.2 to 0.6 kilograms of garbage per head per day. Also, it is a well known fact that land in India is scarce. The garbage collector who comes to your house every morning to empty your dustbins inside his truck, takes all the garbage from your neighborhood and dumps it on an abandoned piece of land. Garbage collectors from all parts of the city meet there to do the same. Such a land is called a landfill. At the end of the day, it is safe to say that all garbage gets dumped in a landfill. Cities those are fortunate enough to have a river passing through them, have an additional dump for all their garbage.

We Indian people also litter excessively. India's per capita waste generation is so high, that it creates a crisis if the garbage collector doesn't visit a neighborhood for a couple of days. The sweeper again sends all this garbage to the local dump, from where it finally goes to a landfill. But, have you ever thought that where would your garbage go ultimately? Improper disposing and burning of waste causes large-scale environmental pollution, which has been spreading day by day. In the present scenario waste management is committed to recycling the wastes because it makes good environmental sense but it is not profitable. Of course, as individuals, we need to realize that we do generate quite a lot of waste – we dispose of containers that can be reused and we throw away papers that can be recycled. It is important to reduce our wastage of resources so that we don't pressurize our weak waste disposal system.

The apathy of a common man towards Mother Earth in general and Environment in particular is mainly responsible for the poor state of aesthetics and health caused due to environmental degradation. As they say "Charity begins at home" is very true here. If we cannot handle a small quantity of waste materials generated in our house and depend on Local Body to take care of it, then dumping yards are bound to be there and environment is going to get degraded further and further.

The waste disposal issues have been given a small attention by the common man, Government and policymakers. This **"National Conference on Waste Disposal and Its Effect on Biodiversity"** had been organized to publicize this burning issue of waste disposal among researchers, academicians and policymakers, so that necessary steps could be taken to get rid of these heaps of wastes. I hope that this proceeding would hit the target to maintain new waste disposal strategies and integrated waste management system in the pace of economy of our country.

—Editors

Acknowledgement

Knowledge is in the end based on Acknowledgement"

Ludwig Wittgenstein

Behind every success there is certainly an unseen power of Almighty. Even if his Kindness couldn't be acknowledged by anyone, though we are immeasurably gratified to Almighty *'God'*, whose gracious blessings enabled us to complete this work.

We are highly thankful to *Department of Science and Technology* (*DST*), *New Delhi* and *UP Council for Science and Technology* (*CST, UP*), *Lucknow* for providing financial support to conduct "National conference on Waste Disposal and Its Effect on Biodiversity".

Words fail us when we depict our profound feeling of gratitude for the people who have rendered individual help during this assignment. Yet, we intend to make a sincere effort in portraying our feelings in the form of words.

We are indebted and express our heartfelt regards to *Honbl'e Mohmmad Azam Khan Sahab*, Founder and Chancellor, Mohmmad Ali Jauhar University, Rampur, whose motivational support, affability, encouragement, excellent supervision and constructive criticism during the entire course have helped us to complete this herculean task.

We are extremely grateful to *Dr. Aziz Qureshi* (Governor of Mizoram), *Prof. Mohd. Yunus* (Vice chancellor, Mohammad Ali Jauhar University) *Dr. Ashwani Kumar Goyal* (Joint Secretary, UP Higher Education, Lucknow), *Dr. Paramatma Singh* (Principal, Govt. Raza PG College, Rampur), *Dr. Sharad P Kale* (Senior Scientist, BARC, Mumbai) *Dr. M.A. Siddiqui*, (Dean, Department of Zoology, Mohmmad Ali Jauhar University) and *Dr. A.K. Saxena* (Govt.

Raza PG College, Rampur) for their encouragement and untiring efforts and to all the participants, our dedicated team of faculty members for their help and co-operation.

We are whole heartedly thankful to *Mr. Pavan Kumar*, Department and Science and Technology, New Delhi and *Dr. M K J Siddiqui*, Director, CST UP, Lucknow for their inspiration and beholden support. Thanks are also due to all contributors and our Publisher "Discovery Publishing House, New Delhi" for playing their part in all view.

In the last but not least we are indeed grateful to our respected and beloved parents, who inspired us at every step and gave us steadfast and unflinching moral support, encouragement and showered packets of selfless love at each and every moment, we would have not achieved this goal without their blessings and support.

Dr. B. Tabassum
Dr. Priya Bajaj
Dr. Pawan Kumar 'Bharti'

Contents

***Pages:* 1-10**

WASTE MANAGEMENT AND ENVIRONMENTAL HEALTH
***Edited by:* Dr. B. Tabassum; Dr. Priya Bajaj & Dr. Pawan Kumar 'Bharti'**
ISBN: 978-93-5056-777-7
***Edition:* 2016**
***Published by:* Discovery Publishing House Pvt. Ltd., New Delhi (India)**

Nisargruna Technology for Urban and Rural Waste Management, Energy Conservation, Better Environment and Restoration of Soil Fertility

Sharad P. Kale

EXECUTIVE SUMMARY

Organic manure is an important component of sustainable agriculture. Indian soils have been productive over several centuries and the organic matter in these soils has perceptibly declined over a period of time. The best way to replenish the organic matter is through the application of organic manure. The biodegradable wastes generated in the kitchens and vegetable markets; and agro-waste generated in agricultural fields are important sources of the organic manure. However these waste materials are to be processed scientifically to obtain good quality manure. The processing of biodegradable waste has proved to be a tricky problem and despite various technologies available worldwide, we have not been able

Agriculture and Biotechnology Division, Bhabha Atomic Research Centre, Mumbai.

Corresponding Author: Nuclear Agriculture and Biotechnology Division, Bhabha Atomic Research Centre, Mumbai (Maharashtra) - 400 085
Email: spkale@gmail.com

to achieve this objective effectively. The NISARGRUNA technology developed by Bhabha Atomic Research centre offers a comprehensive solution for handling the biodegradable waste materials. It is based on the concept of maintaining the elemental balance in the NATURE. The process combines aerobic and anaerobic degradation of the biodegradable waste materials. The aerobic phase is aided by the addition of hot water to support the growth of efficient thermophilic and thermoduric degraders belonging to the Genus *Bacillus*. The anaerobic phase results in formation of biogas and organic manure, which can help in obtaining the self sustainability of the project. The organic manure is rich in nitrogen, carbon, potassium and phosphorous and devoid of any heavy metals. The weed seeds are either macerated in the mixer or killed by the hot water added in the predigester; hence it is weed-free.

The *NISARGRUNA* concept is developed mainly for decentralized processing of the biodegradable waste that would help in reducing the transportation cost and health menace associated with it. It is expected that units of 1, 2, 5 and 10 tons per day capacities would be ideal for urban local bodies in the country. Similar units would also be workable in rural areas for handling the agro waste. The project is expected to generate employment in the downtrodden sector of the society. It would help the ever-depleting energy sector by generating fuel for domestic cooking. The technology has evolved in last 8 years and 190 such NISARGRUNA plants are operative in Maharashtra, Keral, Tamil Nadu, Gujrat, Karnataka, Himachal Pradesh, Jharkhand, Orissa and Delhi.

INTRODUCTION

Two laws govern the Mother Earth. They are - law of conservation of matter and law of conservation of energy. Matter and energy can neither be created nor destroyed. They only change through various forms. The various elemental cycles keep running at a steady pace. The life on earth is part of this cycle. The Life cycle is thus an integration of various elemental cycles. It is important that all these cycles must continue in an undisturbed fashion to maintain the Nature's Cycle. We must look at every material as a potential resource.

The concept of waste therefore needs to be revamped in totality. In fact there is no waste generated in Nature. Every component that is generated is a part of some cycle. Hence each waste should be reused. We must change the name of WASTE BIN to RESOURCE BIN. This will help to change the mental attitude.

The key issues involved in solid waste management are:

- Growth in population and increasing garbage generation
- Segregation of waste at source in as many categories as practical
- Waste collection system
- Scientific processing of the waste materials depending on their nature
- Decentralized means to process waste to avoid multiple transfers and facilitate disposal
- Developing infrastructure for solid waste disposal and processing
- Developing information collection and processing system for solid waste management

NISARGRUNA

The NISARGRUNA (repaying Nature's loan) concept is developed mainly for decentralized processing of the biodegradable waste that would help in reducing the transportation cost and health menace associated with it. It is expected that units of 1, 2, 5 and 10 tonne per day capacities would be ideal for urban local bodies in the country. Similar units would also be workable in rural areas for handling agro-waste. The project is expected to generate employment in the downtrodden sector of the society. It would help the ever-depleting energy sector by generating fuel for domestic cooking. The technology has evolved in last 8 years and more than 160 such NISARGRUNA plants are operative in Maharashtra, Gujrat, Karnataka, Tamil Nadu, Orissa, Kerala, Madhya Pradesh, Jharkhand and Delhi.

SCIENCE OF NISARGRUNA

The waste generated in kitchen in the form of vegetable refuge, stale cooked and uncooked food, extracted tea powder, waste milk and milk products can all be processed in this plant. We have introduced a 3-5 HP mixer to process the waste before putting it into predigester tank. The waste is converted in slurry by mixing with water (1:1) in this mixer. Usually this is the failure point as solid waste is difficult to get digested and can easily clog the system. If we can pulverise the waste in a paste, the digestion is assured. This helps in first stage of methanogenesis viz. hydrolysis. There will be no scum formation and no clogging. The other important thing is use of thermophilic/thermoduric microbes for faster degradation of the waste. The growth of thermophiles in the predigester tank is assured by mixing the waste with hot water and maintaining the temperature in the range of 45-50°C.

The hot water supply is from a solar heater. Even few hours' sunlight is sufficient per day to meet the needs of hot water. Alternately, part of biogas generated in the system can be used for getting hot water. It must be remembered that the reactions in predigester are exothermic in nature and only a proportionate quantum of hot water is needed to achieve the results. Their main role is to digest proteins and low molecular weight carbohydrates to produce volatile fatty acids. Ideally there would be two predigesters which will receive the waste on alternate days so that undisturbed digestion for about 48 hours will give desirable results. The same result can be achieved by providing a baffle wall in single predigester. It is mandatory that the effective volume in either case will be the same. The Ph of the slurry drops to 4 - 6 due to accumulation of volatile fatty acids.

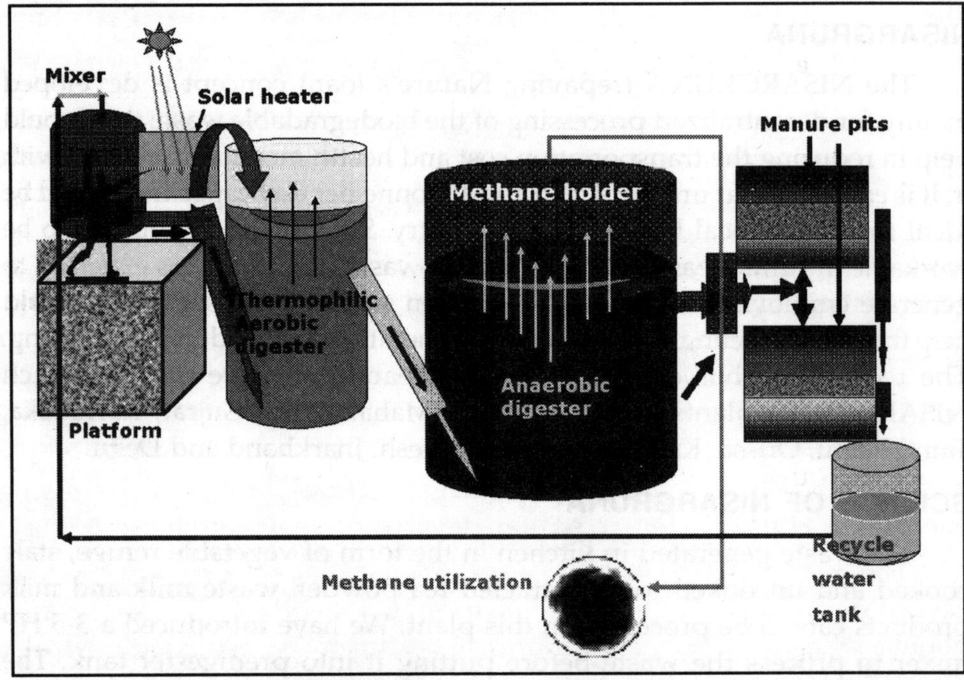

Experimental Plan for Nisargruna

The total soluble solids reduce from 23-25% to 13-15% in this tank. The retention time is between 72 to 96 hours. More retention in predigester than this period would result in loss of biogas and manure in the second phase.

Predigestion is extremely important for following reasons:

- Hydrolysis of the waste
- Acidification and formation of volatile fatty acids

- Removal of scum forming components
- Removal of sulphur in the form of sulphur dioxide
- Formation of uniformly flowable slurry to ensure smooth digestion in anaerobic digester

After the predigester tank the slurry enters the main tank where it undergoes mainly anaerobic degradation by a consortium of archaebacteria belonging to *Methanococcus* group. These bacteria are naturally present in the alimentary canal of ruminant animals (cattle). They produce mainly methane from the cellulosic materials in the slurry. As the gas is generated in the main tank, the dome is slowly lifted up. The design of the dome, which floats on a water seal, is such that there is no direct contact between the slurry and the dome. It reaches a maximum height of 4 feet holding biogas. The biogas is a mixture of methane (55-75%), carbon di oxide (40-15%) and water vapours (5-10%). It is taken through GI pipeline to the lampposts. Drains for condensed water vapour are provided on line. This gas burns with a blue flame and can be used for cooking as well. The excess gas is liberated in the atmosphere after the dome reaches maximum height. The utilization of gas should be spaced in such a manner that this release of excess gas is avoided. The main component in biogas is methane (green house gas) and it has a very high negative impact on the environment. The pressure in the dome is between 100 to 200mm of water column. The pressure is sufficient to take this gas to a distance of about 300-400m without any loss of efficiency. The pressure can be increased by putting additional weight in the form of MS discs or any other suitable and aesthetically acceptable alternative. A gas blower can help in giving the biogas with constant speed and elevated pressure at the user point.

The undigested lignocelluloses and hemicelluloses materials then are passed on in the settling tank in the form of finely divided powder. After about a month high quality manure can be dug out from the settling tanks. There is no odour to the manure at all. The organic contents are high and this can improve the quality of humus in soil, which in turn is responsible for the fertility. The manure can be used for nurseries and fields. The manure pits are provided with filtration system that can separate out the water in an underground tank. This water can be reused in the system. The BOD of this water is less than 70-80. The bucket centrifuge can do the job faster for higher capacity plants.

Nisargruna technology offers an economically viable option for waste disposal. The savings on transportation of waste materials at dumping yards (considering decentralized nature of Nisargruna plants), moderate earning through gas and manure and possible carbon credits can make the technology very attractive. It would also have impacts on health sector.

MONITORING PROCESS

The desirable digestion of heterogeneous biological waste in Nisargruna plant depends on several factors.

- The grinder/mixer/shredder combination has to be used as per the feed quality. Vegetable market waste will need serially operated shredder and mixer while food waste from hotels can be processed by using only mixer.
- The aeration has to be given intermittently at recommended rate so as to maintain the aerobic conditions in the pre-digester continuously.
- Hot water is to be added at recommended rate daily. If solar panels are not functioning due to winter or cloudy days, part of biogas may be used for heating water.
- pH of outgoing slurry from pre-digester into main digester should be between 5-6. If it is too acidic (pH < 5), then the feeding should be halted for a day or two till it recovers to the desirable value.
- If there is any scum formation in the pre-digester, it should be attended to. Aeration at high pressure can help in breaking the scum. Scum formation is mostly due to inefficient grinding. Care must be taken to maintain the mixer blades sharp.
- The processing room should be washer thoroughly with detergents after processing is over. Care must be taken to switch on the fly repellent lamp while processing is going on.
- The exhaust fan in the processing room must be on while processing the waste.
- pH of the main digester slurry flowing into the manure collection pits must always be more than 7. If it is even 6.8, care must be taken to give 2-3 days processing holiday till it recovers to 7 or more. Occasionally gobar can be added at the interval of six months to maintain the good quality of methanogenic culture.
- Biogas must be analyzed using gas chromatographic procedure once a month and record must be maintained. Online methane analyzer may be added to the system if cost is included in the project.
- Manure slurry is to be analyzed for BOD once a month.

- Gas meter has a tendency to get defunct if water enters along with biogas into it. To avoid water in the biogas, water traps have been added in the system. However operator has to make sure that water is removed frequently. Care has been taken in the design to remove maximum water from the biogas, however a close monitoring is a must for avoiding moisture.
- Daily records of the quantity of biogas generated, the quantity of waste processed, pH of main and pre digesters is to be recorded in a recommended format and monthly records need to be sent to BARC for analysis and studies.

DIFFERENCES FROM CONVENTIONAL ANAEROBIC DIGESTER TECHNOLOGY

Nisargruna technology developed for processing of biodegradable solid waste materials generated in kitchens, vegetable market, slaughter houses and animal stables is based on aerobic-anaerobic sequential processes. It offers an excellent alternative for decentralized processing of solid biodegradable waste and avoids the contamination of land-fill sites. It differs from the classical anaerobic digesters in the following aspects:

1. Nisargruna plant has a broader scope to accept a variety of raw materials mentioned above while the anaerobic system developed in our country is mainly used for processing animal dung.
2. Nisargruna technology is a high rate biomethanation process. It uses a mixer to homogenize the biodegradable waste with water into free flowing slurry.
3. Nisargruna process involves pretreatment of the homogenized biodegradable waste slurry in an aerobic digester for a limited period (about 3-4 days). This process is accentuated by aeration and higher temperature. The temperature is maintained between 45-50ºC using solar energy. The hydrolysis and acidification stages are carried out in this phase.
4. Aerobic phase helps in removing scum forming protein materials. This is a major achievement as scum formation can terminate the entire process.
5. It helps in oxidation of sulphur compounds. Formation of hydrogen sulphide is thereby avoided in anaerobic process and biogas formed is free of this corrosive gas.

6. The temperature in this range (45-50°C) helps in hygienization of the waste. All coli-form bacteria are eliminated due to higher temperature and acidic conditions.
7. There are several structural changes made in anaerobic digester. These changes are intended for smoother particle movement and enrichment of biogas with respect to methane value.
8. The dome structure has been changed to avoid its contact with slurry (which used to be the case in gobar gas technology) thereby ensuring proper entrapment of the biogas.
9. The water coming out of the anaerobic slurry is allowed to settle in settling tanks where filtration is used to remove manure and recycle the water.
10. Thus the plant achieves the dream of "Zero garbage, Zero effluent and Zero energy process" as more energy is generated in the form of biogas than energy spent in the operation of the plant.
11. It has a good potential to generate the employment opportunities in lower strata of the society. The NGOs of such dedicated persons can help in achieving this target.
12. The manure generated in the process is weed-free and rich in organic carbon contents. Hence it will be a better soil conditioner than any other organic manure.
13. The biogas has better fuel value. It can be used for thermal purpose or can be converted to electricity.
14. The technology can be upgraded as per user's requirement. This is especially useful in urban area where large quantities of wastes are generated in relatively smaller places.

ADVANTAGES OF NISARGRUNA TECHNOLOGY

1. Environmental friendly processing of biodegradable waste is achieved. This waste is completely zeroed and by-products are generated.
2. The elemental cycles like nitrogen, carbon, hydrogen, oxygen etc. cycles expect that the biodegradable waste has to go through microbial route for ensuring their availability for future life. Nisargruna achieves this objective fully.
3. The processing cost of biodegradable waste is far lesser compared to any other foreign technology.

4. Decentralized handling of the waste will reduce the transportation costs, dumping yard needs and assured processing. In long run, it means that dumping yards could be totally eliminated. If proper segregation occurs at the source, then the requirement of land-fill sites can be reduced by 60-70%.
5. Transportation of this waste through crowded areas could easily be avoided if decentralized Nisargruna plants are made available.
6. By-products like biogas and manure can make the process economically attractive.
7. Processing of solid biodegradable waste in this manner would ensure that this material won't be carried to dumping yards and release methane there, in slow and unplanned composting. Since the biogas is trapped to burn, the contamination of environment with a vast quantity of methane will be completely avoided. This would earn carbon credit.
8. The use of biogas as fuel will save the classical fuel consumption including petrol, LPG and diesel. This is another reason which will ensure the carbon credit for the process.
9. In rural areas where biomass can be made available to run these plants, energy-freedom can easily be achieved. The stand-alone Nisargruna plants can be rural power houses.
10. In rural areas it will reduce the use of wood as fuel thereby helping indirectly in afforestation.
11. The aesthetic looks of the country can be changed using Nisargruna technology.
12. It offers a long-life methodology to treat the biodegradable waste in a very limited space. The continuity of the process makes it possible to treat a large quantity of waste at a single site without any need of adjoining areas.
13. The technology is relatively simple and does not involve any imports. The plants can be operated by unskilled workers after training them initially for about 3-4 weeks. It is developed keeping in mind local environment and the types of wastes.
14. The manure generated in the process will help in rejuvenating the depleting organic carbon contents in our agricultural soils.
15. The processing of biodegradable waste and making it zero would tremendously improve the hygiene of the country, reduce the

epidemics and make people in general healthy. The substantial reduction in health bills is a distinct possibility. It would also influence the human efficiency.

ECONOMICS OF THE NISARGRUNA PROCESS

Nisargruna concept offers a technology which helps in:

1. Decentralized processing of biodegradable waste.
2. Achieving the dream of zero garbage and zero effluent.
3. Reduction in transportation costs.
4. Maintenance of biogeochemical elemental cycles.
5. Generation of by-products which can give financial support and motivation for the operators.
6. Employment generation in lower economic strata of society.
7. Reduction in dumping yard menace.
8. Quality improvement in dry waste as the wet and degradable portion is removed from that.
9. Benefits in carbon credits.
10. Benefits in health sector.

Pages: **11-26**

WASTE MANAGEMENT AND ENVIRONMENTAL HEALTH
Edited by: **Dr. B. Tabassum; Dr. Priya Bajaj & Dr. Pawan Kumar 'Bharti'**
ISBN: 978-93-5056-777-7
Edition: **2016**
Published by: **Discovery Publishing House Pvt. Ltd., New Delhi (India)**

Sources, Effects and Management of Aquatic Toxicants

B. Tabassum and **Priya Bajaj**

INTRODUCTION

Environmental toxicology is a multidisciplinary field of environmental science concerned with the study of the harmful effects of various chemical, biological and physical agents on living organisms, change in the health of individuals or indirect effects by disrupting or defiling the content of lakes, oceans, forests, and the atmosphere. Environmental toxicology is a young field that has developed rapidly over the past 40 years. It involves the studying of sources, pathways, transformations, and effects of chemicals that are harmful in the environment.

Department of Zoology, Govt. Raza PG College, Rampur (UP) - 244 901
Corresponding Author: Priya Bajaj, Department of Zoology, Govt. Raza PG College, Rampur (UP) - 244 901, *Email:* drpriyabajaj73@gmail.com
Mob.: +91 - 9411045931

Point Sources of Environmental Toxicants to Water Bodies

Although we're taught we should make sure we get plenty of nutrients in our daily diet, environmental toxicology has found evidence that an excess amount of nutrients in runoff from agricultural fields can devastate an aquatic system. Although phosphorous, carbon and nitrogen are essential to proper growth, too much of them can cause a harmful surplus of plant and microbial growth that can choke and kill ecological systems. This causes eutrophication in lakes and streams, which is usually the reason behind massive fish kills. Environmental toxicologists investigate these kinds of habitat disruptions and advise on how to resolve them. Since the industrial revolution of more than 150 years ago, consumer and factory waste products, which erode soils and release heavy metals into our natural water supply, have rapidly contaminated our drinking water. Environmental toxicology researches the amount and effects of these metallic elements that are considered high density and toxic to humans in minimal doses. Some of the more common heavy metals are mercury, arsenic, lead, and chromium, which can accumulate in our bodies. Creating substances that can counteract the effects of these metals is another facet of environmental toxicology.

Organisms can be introduced to toxicants at various stages of their life cycle. The degree of toxicity can vary depending on where the organism is found within its food web. Bioaccumulation occurs when molecular compounds are stored in an organism's fatty tissues. Over time, this leads to the establishment of a trophic cascade and the *biomagnification* of specific toxicants. Harmful effects of chemical and biological agents can include toxicants from pollutants, insecticides, pesticides, and fertilizers all of which can impact an organism and its community. Legislation has been implemented since the early 1970s to ensure that harmful effects of environmental toxicants are minimized for all species. Unfortunalety, according to *McCarty (2013)* we are facing the risk of entering in a "dark age" due to longstanding limitations in the implementation of the simple conceptual modes.

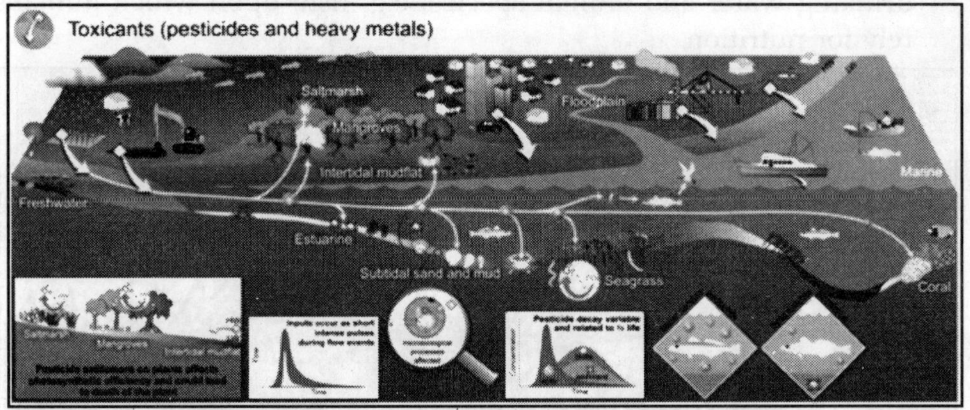

Sources of Environmental Toxicants (Water Borne)

There are many sources of environmental toxicity that can lead to the presence of toxicants in our food, water and air:

1. **Heavy metals:** Heavy metals like mercury, lead, aluminum and cadmium are found in food sources, such as fish can also have harmful effects. Metals released from mining and industrial processes are among the major contaminants in aquatic environments. Mercury, the most toxic, is also released into the atmosphere from burning coal, where it can be transported long distances before being deposited far from its source. In addition to numerous experimental studies in laboratory animals, there is epidemiological evidence, like *Minamata* (Mass mercury poisoning) and *Itai-itai* (Mass Cadmium poisoning) tragedy of Japan. The town of Minamata Japan, where in the 1950s and 60s a factory discharged Hg into the bay from which people ate fish that had accumulated the contaminant, was a site of Hg poisoning of the human population. Also in the Toyoma town of Japan rice fields became house for Itai-itai disease.

2. **Pesticides:** Pesticides are a major source of environmental toxicity. These chemically synthesized agents have been known to persist in the environment long after their administration. The poor biodegradability of pesticides can result in bioaccumulation of chemicals in various organisms along with *biomagnification* within a food web. Pesticides can be categorized according to the pests they target. Insecticides are used to eliminate agricultural pests that attack

various fruits and crops. Herbicides target herbal pests such as weeds and other unwanted plants that reduce crop production. Pesticides, as well as fertilizers, can infiltrate water sources – contaminating drinking water and animal species, e.g. fish, upon which humans rely for nutrition.

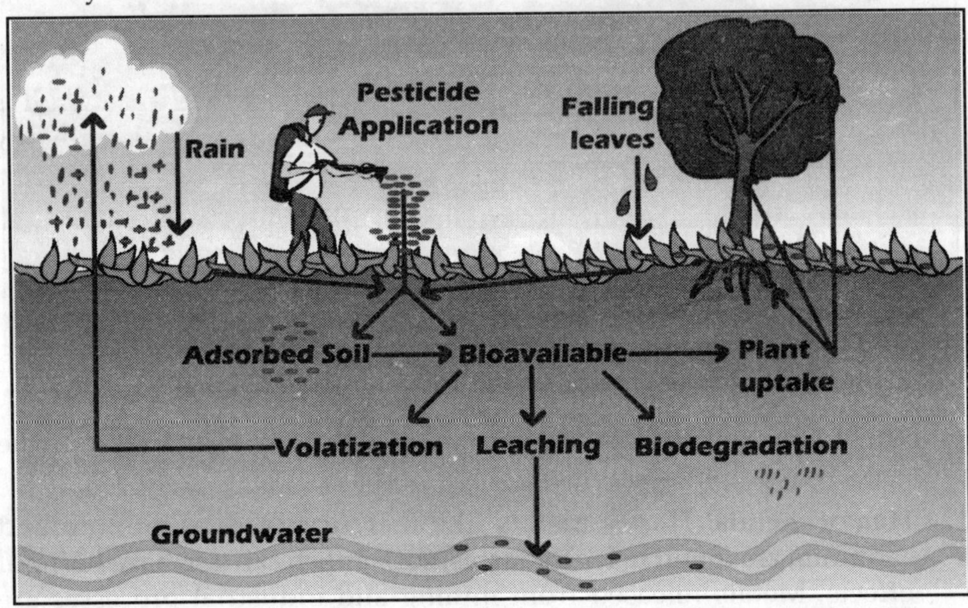

Dichlorodiphenyltrichloroethane (DDT) is an organochlorine insecticide that has been banned due to its adverse effects on both humans and wildlife. DDT was widely used by farmers in order to kill agricultural pests such as the potato beetle, coddling moth and corn earworm. DDT is not easily biodegradable and thus the chemical accumulates in soil and sediment runoff. Water systems become polluted and marine life such as fish and shellfish accumulate DDT in their tissue [Clarkson, 1992] Furthermore, this effect is amplified when animals who consume the fish also consume the chemical. Humans who consume animals or plants that are contaminated with DDT experience adverse health effects. Various studies have shown that DDT has damaging effects on the liver, nervous system and reproductive system of humans.

3. **PCBs:** Polychlorinated biphenyls (PCBs) are organic pollutants that are still present in our environment today despite being banned in many countries such as the United States and Canada. Due to the persistent nature of PCBs in aquatic ecosystems, many aquatic species like fish farmed salmon contain high levels of this chemical. Due to

their stability, non-flammability, and insulating properties, PCBs were used in hundreds of industrial processes, some of which are electrical, heat transfer, and hydraulic equipment. They entered the environment accidentally during their manufacture and use, and because of their persistence, still remain in aquatic sediments decades after their use has ceased.

4. **Chloroform:** This colorless liquid has a pleasant, nonirritating odour and a slightly sweet taste, and is used to make other chemicals. It is formed when chlorine is added to water for purification. It primarily affects the human liver.

5. **VOCs (Volatile Organic Compounds):** Major sources of VOCs in drinking water are, carpet, paints, deodorants, cleaning fluids, varnishes, cosmetics, dry cleaned clothing, moth repellants. They cause Cancer, eye and respiratory tract irritation, headaches, dizziness, visual disorders, and memory impairment.

6. **Dioxins:** These are the chemical compounds formed as a result of combustion processes such as commercial or municipal waste incineration and from burning fuels (like wood, coal or oil). Over 95 percent of human exposure comes from eating commercial animal fats like fish. Dioxins are persistent contaminant that are very toxic at very low concentrations. They were never manufactured on purpose, but were byproducts of manufacture of some herbicides, and is produced by burning plastics and in paper mills.

7. **Acid Rain:** Acid rain is an outcome of air pollution ultimately affecting water bodies. It decreases the pH of water bodies, affects the buildings and causes skin problems.

8. **Flame Retardants:** Poly brominated diphenyl ethers (PBDE) are commonly used as flame retardants in furniture and other household products. They are persistent and lipophilic and likely to accumulate in sediments and to be biomagnified up food webs. High levels have been detected in wildlife.

9. **Pharmaceuticals and Personal Care Products:** Pharmaceuticals get into the aquatic environment because they are not removed by current technology in sewage treatment plants. Pharmaceuticals are designed to produce effects at very low concentrations, so they affect aquatic biota such as fishes as well as humans.

10. **Phthalates:** Plastic wrap, plastic bottles disposed in water bodies contain Phthalates. These chemicals are used to lengthen the life of fragrances and soften plastics.

11. **Oil and Hydrocarbons:** Petroleum hydrocarbons have been a long-standing problem in the marine environment due to oil spills and the resultant mortality of large numbers of birds and marine mammals. When exposed to the air, oil undergoes a process called –weathering, in which some volatile components evaporate and some components are degraded by sunlight or microbes. The chemical composition and physical characteristics of the oil change due to these processes. The sequestered oil does not weather, and weathered oil can still be toxic.

AQUATIC TOXICITY TESTS

Aquatic toxicology tests (assays) are used to provide qualitative and quantitative data on adverse (deleterious) effects on organisms from a toxicant. Toxicity tests can be used to assess the potential for damage to an aquatic environment and provide a database that can be used to assess the risk associated within a situation for a specific toxicant. Aquatic toxicology tests can be performed in the field or in the laboratory. Field experiments generally refer to multiple species exposure and laboratory experiments generally refer to single species exposure. A dose response relationship is most commonly used to quantify the toxic effects at a selected end-point or criteria for effect. The criteria for effects, or endpoints tested for, can include lethal and sublethal effects.

There are different types of toxicity tests that can be performed on various test species. Different species differ in their susceptibility to chemicals, most likely due to differences in accessibility, metabolic rate, excretion rate, genetic factors, dietary factors, age, sex, health and stress level of the organism. As defined by ASTM, these species are routinely selected on the basis of availability, commercial, recreational, and ecological importance, past successful use, and regulatory use. Common standard test species are:

- Fathead minnow (*Pimephales promelas*)
- Daphnids (*Daphnia magna, D. pulex, D. pulicaria, Ceriodaphnia dubia*)
- Midge (*Chironomus tentans, C. ruparius*)
- Rainbow trout (*Oncorhynchus mykiss*)
- Sheepshead minnow (*Cyprinodon variegatu*)
- Mysids (Mysidopsis), oyster (Crassotreas)
- Scud (*Hyalalla azteca*)
- Grass shrimp (*Palaemonetes pugio*)
- Mussels (Mytilus)

A variety of acceptable standardized test methods have been widely accepted in the scientific literature and regulatory agencies. The type of test used depends on many factors: Specific regulatory agency conducting the test, resources available, physical and chemical characteristics of the environment, type of toxicant, test species available, laboratory vs. field testing, end-point selection, and time and resources available to conduct the assays are some of the most common influencing factors on test design.

EFFECTS OF WATERBORNE ENVIRONMENTAL TOXICANTS

Toxicity can be broken down into two broad categories of direct and indirect toxicity. Direct toxicity results from a toxicant acting at the site of action in or on the organism. Indirect toxicity occurs with a change in the physical, chemical, or biological environment. There are a number of effects that occur when an organism is simultaneously exposed to two or more toxicants. These effects include (*Rand etal., 1985*):

- **Additive Effects:** An additive effect occurs when combined effect is equal to a combination or sum of the individual effects.
- **synergistic Effects:** A synergistic effect occurs when the combination of effects is much greater than the two individual effects added together.
- **Potentiation Effects:** Potentiation is an effect that occurs when an individual chemical has no effect is added to a toxicant and the combination has a greater effect than just the toxicant alone.
- **Antagonistic Effects**: An antagonistic effect occurs when a combination of chemicals has less of an effect than the sum of their individual effects.

Lethality is most common effect used in toxicology and used as an endpoint for acute toxicity tests. While conducting chronic toxicity tests sub-lethal effects are endpoints that are looked at. These endpoints include behavioral, physiological, biochemical, histological changes. Effects of various waterborne toxicants can be explained under following headings:

1. **Acute Poisoning:** Acute exposure to pesticides can lead to death or serious illness. Unintentional poisonings kill an estimated 355 000 people globally each year (WHO, 1990). In developing countries – where two thirds of these deaths occur – such poisonings are associated strongly with excessive exposure to, and inappropriate use of, toxic chemicals. In many such settings, toxic chemicals may be emitted directly into water bodies– from industrial processes, pulp and paper plants, tanning operations, mining, and unsustainable forms of

agriculture – at levels or rates well in excess of those tolerable to human health (World Bank, 2002 and UNDP, 1998). In developing countries, deaths by unintentional poisoning may be strongly associated with inappropriate use and poor environmental management of toxic chemicals, including pesticides.

2. **DNA Mutations:** Radioactive toxicants can cause changes at genetic level or DNA mutation that may carry the effects till generations. An example of this type of research involves the detrimental consequences on human health resulting from the radioactive fallout following the Chernobyl nuclear reactor disaster.
3. **The Big C- Cancer:** A major area of research in the field of environmental toxicology involves how toxic elements released into the environment precipitate the emergence of cancers such as leukemia, lung cancer, lymphomas, and melanoma. Some of these harmful chemicals include pesticides, asbestos, solvents, and herbicides. According to the Environmental Protection Agency (EPA), 60 per cent of herbicides, 90 per cent of fungicides and 30 per cent of insecticides are known to be carcinogenic. Pesticide residues have been detected in 50 per cent to 95 per cent of foods. The creation of chemicals meant to facilitate our lives sometimes backfires.
4. **Effects on Reproduction:** Some insecticides, drugs, natural compounds and industrial effluents contain chemicals or chemical mixtures with 'estrogenic' activity, that may affect both male and female reproductive performance. Environmental pollutants that exhibit 'estrogenic' action include some organochlorine insecticides such as chlordecone, DDT and its metabolites, some phthalate plasticizers and some industrial chemicals such as nonylphenol, bisphenol and PCBs.
5. **Effects on Behaviour:** Exposures during certain stages of development may be particularly sensitive. Since behavior is a link between underlying physiological/biochemical processes and an animal's ecology, it is a particularly important type of response for animals in the field. Exposure to some chemicals during early life stages can produce behavioral changes that are manifested later.
6. **Skin Disorders:** Waterborne toxicants like Dioxins causes a number of skin disorders like chloracne (a severe skin disease with acne-like lesions), skin rashes, skin discoloration, excessive body hair etc.
7. **Liver and Kidney Damage:** Chemicals like Chloroform and heavy metals specially Cadmium cause pathological, physiological and biochemical damage to liver and kidneys.

8. **Neurological disorders**: Heavy metals like arsenic, mercury, lead, aluminum and cadmium, which are prevalent in many areas of our environment, can accumulate in soft tissues of the body. They cause neurological disorders like Alzheimer's disease, foggy head, brain damage, mental retardation, psychomotor retardation, cerebral palsy, fatigue, nausea and vomiting etc. Lead (Pb) is a well known neuro-toxicant.
9. **Hematological disorders**: Heavy metals are also responsible for decreased production of red and white blood cells, abnormal heart rhythm, damage to blood vessels.
10. **Endocrine System Damage:** A number of chemicals like phthalates and PBDE may cause endocrine system damage. phthalates chemically mimic hormones and are particularly dangerous to children.
11. **Congenital Disorders:** A number of environmental toxins have potential adverse effects on the prenatal development of both the embryo or fetus, as well as pregnancy complications. The human embryo or fetus is relatively susceptible to impact from adverse conditions within the mother's environment. Sub-par fetal conditions often cause various degrees of developmental delays, both physical and mental, for the growing baby. Such toxins include polychlorinated biphenyls, organochlorine pesticides, perfluorinated compounds, phenols, polybrominated diphenyl ethers, phthalates, polycyclic aromatic hydrocarbons, perchlorate PBDEs, compounds used as flame retardants, and dichlorodiphenyltrichloroethane (DDT) etc. Environmental toxins can show effects such as structural abnormalities, altered growth, functional deficiencies, congenital neoplasia, or even death for the fetus.
12. **Effects on Aquatic Fauna:** It has been shown that fish like rainbow trout are exposed to higher cadmium levels and grow at a slower rate. Moreover, cadmium can potentially alter the productivity and mating behaviours of these fish. Acid rain decreases the pH of water bodies. It also increases the mobility of aluminium of soil to waterbodies. Combination of these two impair development of gill in fishes. Fluoride has been known to negatively affect aquatic wildlife. Elevated levels of fluoride have been proven to impair the feeding efficiency and growth of the common carp. Exposure to fluoride alters nutritional value of fishes.
13. **Effects on genetic diversity:** Heavy metals can affect the genetic makeup in aquatic organisms. Some aquatic species have evolved heavy metal tolerances.

MANAGEMENT OF WATERBORNE TOXICANTS

Management of waterborne toxicants includes three steps- Avoiding Exposure, Monitoring toxicants and Their control.

A. **Avoiding Exposure:** It's impossible in this day and age to avoid all environmental toxins. What you can do, however, is limit your exposure as much as possible with the following tips:

- Buy and eat, as much as possible, organic produce and free-range, organic foods. If you can only purchase one organic product it probably should be free range organic eggs.
- Rather than eating fish, which is largely contaminated with PCBs and mercury, consume a high-quality purified fish or cod liver oil. Another option is to have your wild-caught fish lab tested to find out if it is a pure source.
- Avoid processed foods — remember that they're processed with chemicals.
- Only use natural cleaning products in your home.
- Switch over to natural brands of toiletries, including shampoo, toothpaste, antiperspirants and cosmetics.
- Remove any metal fillings as they're a major source of mercury. Be sure to have this done by a qualified biological dentist.
- Avoid using artificial air fresheners, dryer sheets, fabric softeners or other synthetic fragrances as they can pollute the air you are breathing.
- Avoid artificial food additives of all kind, including artificial sweeteners and MSG.
- Get plenty of safe sun exposure to boost your vitamin D levels and your immune system, so that you will be better able to fight disease.

B. **Monitoring toxicants:** For any potential environmental hazard one of the main principles for monitoring and control is to identify the critical agents, pathways and populations at risk. Such considerations will guide the methods to be used for monitoring and surveillance. Monitoring (routine measurements aimed at detecting changes in the environment or health) can use data from a range of sources, including:

- Records of the permitted or actual level of emissions from specified sources.

- Measurements of the concentrations of pollutants in the environment.
- Measurements of specific agents or their metabolic products in biological samples.
- Health data Routine (surveillance) data
- Clinical surveillance (relevant to specific exposed populations)
- Infectious disease monitoring data
- Health care utilization data (hospital admissions, primary care consultations)
- Births, congenital anomalies and related data
- Cancer registrations
- Mortality statistics
- Epidemiological surveys.

C. **Control of Waterborne Toxicants:** Control of environmental hazards depends on:

- Defining acceptable levels of exposure and hence health risk.
- Taking a precautionary approach in the absence of clear evidence.
- Determining the levels of control to keep exposure below the specified thresholds.
- Licensing/banning specific substances (e.g. PCBs)
- Setting of emissions controls (e.g. industrial effluent discharge)
- Enforcement of concentrations or exposure limits for specific target groups
- Enforcement of health and safety protection
- Setting of guidelines/standards relating to environmental levels (e.g. Standard permissible limits in drinking water).

These may be implemented by voluntary agreement, balance of penalties and benefits to encourage good practice and dissuade bad, legal mandate. Measures which entail licensing, emissions control, or health and safety protection, can be enforced on individuals or individual companies. Guidelines and standards relating to general environmental levels do not entail direct influence over the polluters. Quality standards are set for the physical, chemical and biological characteristics of drinking water and monitored throughout the water treatment and distribution network through to the household tap. Control measures for toxicant exposure can be applied at following levels:

- **In the Field:** Integrated Pest Management (IPM) strategies can reduce the use of agrochemicals, improve management, and optimize ecosystem mechanisms for pest control/soil enrichment – simultaneously protecting both farmers and the environment.
- **At the National Level:** Policies to improve regulation and control of pesticide and other chemical sale, distribution, and use; health care systems to identify, treat, and monitor cases of acute poisonings; and educational/advocacy tools to inform the public as well as agriculture and health-care workers about health risks and best practice use of agrochemicals – all are important.
- **At the Global Level:** Implementation of global conventions on the management of highly toxic chemicals, including certain pesticides, from production to disposal stages is also critical. These include: the Stockholm Convention on Persistent Organic Pollutants; the Rotterdam Convention on Prior Informed Consent Procedure for Certain Hazardous Chemicals in International Trade, and the Basel Convention on the Control of Transboundary Movements of Hazardous Waste and their Disposal (World Bank, 2003).

Some Important societies for the management of waterborne toxicants are as following:

- **American Society for Testing and Materials (ASTM International):** A consensus organization, representing 135 countries, that develops and delivers international voluntary standard methods for aquatic toxicity testing.
- **Standard Methods for the Examination of Water and Wastewater:** A compilation of techniques for the examination of water, jointly published by the American Public Health Association (APHA), the American Water Works Association (AWWA), and the Water Pollution Control Federation (WPCF).
- **Ecotox:** A database maintained by the U.S. Environmental Protection Agency (EPA) that offers single chemical toxicity information for both aquatic and terrestrial purposes.
- **Society of Environmental Toxicology and Chemistry (SETAC):** A nonprofit, worldwide society working to promote scientific research to further our understanding of environmental stressors, environmental education, and the use of science in environmental policy.

- **United States Environmental Protection Agency (USEPA):** A federal agency working to protect human and environmental health. Among many other functions, the U.S. EPA produces guidance manuals outlining aquatic toxicity test procedures.
- **Organization for Economic Co-operation and Development (OECD):** A forum for governments to work together to promote policies for the betterment of people's social and economic well-being around the world. One way in which they accomplish this is through the development of aquatic toxicity test guidelines.
- **Environment Canada (EC):** A diverse organization working to protect Canada's water resources and the natural environment through the coordination of environmental policies and programmes with the federal government.[9]

Some common terminology used to define monitoring and control of waterborne environmental toxicants are described as below (*Rand etal., 1985*):

- **Median Lethal Concentration (LC50):** The chemical concentration that is expected to kill 50% of a group of organisms.
- **Median Effective Concentration (EC50):** The chemical concentration that is expected to have one or more specified effects in 50% of a group of organisms.
- **Critical Body Residue (CBR):** An approach that routinely examines whole-body chemical concentrations of an exposed organism that is associated with an adverse biological response.
- **Baseline toxicity:** Refers to narcosis which is a depression in biological activity due to toxicants being present in the organism.
- **Biomagnification:** The process by which the concentration of a chemical in the tissues of an organism increases as it passes through several levels in the food web.
- **Lowest Observed Effect Concentration (LOEC):** The lowest test concentration that has a statistically significant effect over a specified exposure time.
- **No Observed Effect Concentration (NOEC):** The highest test concentration for which no effect is observed relative to a control over a specified exposure time.
- **Maximum Acceptable Toxicant Concentrations (MATC):** An estimated value that represents the highest "no-effect" concentration of a specific substance within the range including the NOEC and LOEC.

- **Application Factor (AF):** An empirically derived "safe" concentration of a chemical.
- **Biomonitoring:** The consistent use of living organisms to analyze environmental changes over time.
- **Effluent:** Liquid, industrial discharge that usually contain varying chemical toxicants.
- **Quantitative Structure-Activity Relationship (QSAR):** A method of modeling the relationship between biological activity and the structure of organic chemicals.
- **Mode of Action:** A set of common behavioral or physiological signs that represent a type of adverse response.
- **Mechanism of Action:** The detailed events that take place at the molecular level during an adverse biological response.
- **KOW:** The octanol-water partition coefficient which represents the ratio of the concentration of octanol to the concentration of chemical in the water.
- **Bioconcentration Factor (BCF):** The ratio of the average chemical concentration in the tissues of the organism under steady-state conditions to the average chemical concentration measured in the water to which the organisms are exposed.

REFERENCES

1. A. Carpi, The Toxicology of Mercury, National Science Foundation - Vision Learning, New York, April 5, 2001.
2. Amiard-Triquet, C. Behavioural Disturbances: The Missing Link Between Sub-organismal and Supra-organismal Responses to Stress? Prospects Based on Aquatic Research. Hum. Ecol. Risk Assess. 2009, 15, 87-110.
3. Bickham J.W., Sandhu S., Hebert P.D., Chikhi L., and Athwal R. (2000). "Effects of Chemical Contaminants on Genetic Diversity in Natural Populations: Implications for Biomonitoring and Ecotoxicology." Mutat Res. 463.1: 33-51.
4. Bourret, V., Couture, P., Campbell, P.G.C., and Bernatchez, L. (2008). "Evolutionary Ecotoxicology of Wild Yellow Perch (Perca Flavescens) Populations Chronically Exposed to a Polymetallic Gradient." Aquatic Toxicology. 86: 76-90.
5. D. Jolley, G. O'Brien and J. Morrison, Evolution of Chemical Contaminant and Toxicology Studies, Part 1 - An OD. Jolley, G. O'Brien and J. Morrison, Evolution of Chemical Contaminant and Toxicology Studies, Part 1 - An Overview, South Pacific Journal of Natural Science, Vol 21, 1-5.
6. E. Ostad and G.J. Wise, Celestial Bodies and Urinary Stones: Isaac Newton (1641-1727) – Health and Urological Problems BJU International V. 95, No 1, 24-26, 2005.

7. Eroschenko, V.P., 1982. Surface Changes in Oviduct, Uterus and Vaginal Cells of Neonatal Mice after Estradiol-17 Beta and the Insecticide Chlordecone (Kepone) Treatment: A Scanning Electron Microscopic Study. Bio. Repro. 26, 707-720.

8. Eroschenko, V.P., 1985. Morphological Analysis of Chlorodecone (Kepone) Action in Different Mouse Organs: Choroid Plexus in Adult Males and Vaginal Epithelium in Suckling Neonates. In: McLachlan, J.A. (Ed.), Estrogens in the Environment. Elsevier/North Holland, New York, pp. 86-101.

9. Eroschenko, V.P., Palmer, R.D., 1980. Estrogenicity of Kepone in Birds and Mammals. In: McLachlan, J.A. (Ed.), Estrogens in the Environment. Elsevier, New York, pp. 305-325.

10. Food and Agriculture Organization of the United Nations/United Nations Environment Programme/World Health Organization. Childhood Pesticide Poisoning: Information for Advocacy and Action. Geneva, United Nations Environment Programme, 2004.

12. Fry, D.M., Toone, C.K., 1981. DDT-induced Feminization of Gull Embryos. Science 213, 922-924.

12. Gray, L.E., 1992. Chemical-induced Alterations of Sexual Differentiation: A Review of Effects in Humans and Rodents. In: Colborn, T., Clement, C. Jr (Eds.), Chemical-induced Alterations in Sexual and Functional Development: The wildlife/human connection. Princeton Scientific, Princeton, NJ, pp. 203-224.

13. H A Waldron, Did the Mad Hatter have Mercury Poisoning? British Medical Journal Volume 287 24-31 December 1983 1961.

14. Human Development Report – Consumption for Human Development. New York/Oxford, United Nations Development Programme, 1998.

15. J. Patočka, K. Černý, Inorganic Lead Toxicology,Acta Medica (Hradec Kralove), V. 46, No 2, 65-72, 2003.

16. Jobling, S., Sheahan, D., Osborne, J.A., Marthiessen, P., Sumpter, J.P., 1996. Inhibition of Testicular Growth in Rainbow Trout (Oncorhynchus mykiss) Exposed to Estrogenic Alkylphenol Chemicals. Environ. Toxicol. Chem. 15, 194-202.

17. Jobling, S., Sumpter, J.P., 1993. Detergent Components in Sewage Effluents are Weakly Estrogenic to Fish—an *in vitro* Study Using Rainbow Trout (Onchorynchus mykiss) Hepatocytes. Aquat. Toxicol. 27, 361-372.

18. Korach, K.S., Sarver, P., Chae, K., McLachlan, J.A., McKinney, J.D., 1987. Estrogen Receptor-binding Activity of Polychlorinated hydroxybiphenals: Conformationally Restricted Structural Probes. Mol. Pharmacol. 33, 120-126.

19. Krishaan, A.V., Stathis, P., Permuth, S.F., Tokes, L., 1993. Bishphenol A: An Estrogenic Substance is Released from Polycarbonate Flasks during Autoclaving. Endocrinology 132, 2279-2286.

20. Lars D. Hylander, The Rise and Fall of Mercury: Converting a Resource to Refuse After 500 Years of Mining and Pollution, Critical Reviews in Environmental Science and Technology, 341-36, 2005.

21. Lars D. Hylander, Global Mercury Pollution and its Expected Decrease After a Mercury Trade Ban, Water, Air, and Soil Pollution, Vol. 125, 331-344, 2001.

22. Leonard J. Goldwater, Mercury: A History of Quicksilver, York Press, Baltimore, MD, 1972.

23. Lye, C.M., Frid, C.L.J., Gill, M.E., McCormick, D., 1997. Abnormalities in the Reproductive Health of Flounder Platichtys Flesus Exposed to Effluent from a Sewage Treatment Works. Mar. Pollut. Bull. 3, 34-41.

24. McCarty, L.S. (Dec 2013). "Are We in the Dark Ages of Environmental Toxicology?". *Regul Toxicol Pharmacol*. 67 (3): 321-324.

25. Persistent Organic Pollutants: A Legacy of Environmental Harm and Threats to Health. Washington, DC, World Bank, May 2003 (Environment Strategy Series, No. 6).

26. Public Health Impact of Pesticides Used in Agriculture. Geneva, World Health Organization, 1990.

27. Rand, Gary M.; Petrocelli, Sam R. (1985). *Fundamentals of Aquatic Toxicology: Methods and Applications*. Washington: Hemisphere Publishing. ISBN 0-89116-382-4.

28. Sharpe, R.M., Skakkbaek, N.E., 1993. Are Oestrogens Involved in Falling Sperm Counts and Disorders of the Male Reproductive Tract? Lancet 341, 1392-1395.

29. Soto, A.M., Justicia, H., Wray, J.W., Sonnenschein, C., 1991. p-Nonylphenol: An Estrogenic Xenobiotic Released from Modified Polystyrene. Environ. Health Perspect. 92, 167.

30. The State of the Environment: Freshwater. GEO-2000: Global Environment Outlook. Nairobi, United Nations Environment Programme, 1999.

31. Toxics and Poverty: The Impact of Toxic Substances on the Poor in Developing Countries. Washington, DC, World Bank, 2002.

32. United Nations. Development Programme (*UNDP*), 1998; Human Development Report, Oxford University Press, New York.

33. Weis, J.S.; Smith, G.; Zhou, T.; Santiago-Bass, C.; Weis, P. Effects of Contaminants on Behavior: Biochemical Mechanisms and Ecological Consequences. BioScience 2001, 51, 209-217.

34. World Health Organization (WHO), 2000; The World Health Report - Health Systems: Improving Performance.

35. World Bank 2002, World Development Report: Building Institutions for Markets; Oxford University Press, September 2001 (ISBN: 978-0-8213-5016-4)

36. Yáñez L et al. Overview of Human Health and Chemical Mixtures: Problems Facing Developing Countries. Environmental Health Perspectives, 2002, 110(6): 901-909.

Pages: 27-36

WASTE MANAGEMENT AND ENVIRONMENTAL HEALTH

***Edited by:* Dr. B. Tabassum; Dr. Priya Bajaj & Dr. Pawan Kumar 'Bharti'**

ISBN: 978-93-5056-777-7

***Edition:* 2016**

***Published by:* Discovery Publishing House Pvt. Ltd., New Delhi (India)**

Solid Waste Management to Safeguard Environment and Human Health

Pardeep Kumar[1] and Parveen Kumar[2]

INTRODUCTION

Rapid urbanization and industrialization for economic growth are leading to waste generation which is adversely affecting the environment and human health. The waste food and other materials were simply thrown on roads, unpaved streets, and vacant land in ancient towns, leading to their accumulation. The first law inhibiting this practice was established in Athens around 320 B.C. This resulted in evolution of a system for waste removal in various eastern Mediterranean cities. The crude waste disposal methods were used at that time i.e. open pits outside the city (Bharucha, 2004). This practice resulted in increase in population of rodents

[1]Department of Education (B.Ed.), Govt. Raza P.G. College, Rampur, U.P., (India).

[2]Department of Environmental Sciences, Amity School of Earth and Environmental Sciences, Amity University Haryana, Gurgaon (Manesar) – 122 413, Haryana, (India)

Corresponding Author: Dr. Pradeep Kumar, Department of B. Ed., Govt. Raza PG College, Rampur (UP)-244 901, *Email:* pradeepdeengwal78@gmail.com *Mob.* +91 9458912150

and flies which are carriers of germs and pathogenic bacteria. It resulted in outbreak of diseases i.e. plague and claimed many lives. In addition to this, improper solid waste management adversely affects the environment. The waste may contain carcinogenic and bio-recalcitrant substances, i.e. plastics, medicines, pesticides, paints etc., which may dissolve in rain water to form a coloured liquid called leachate. Leachate containing highly toxic organic compounds, e.g. chlorinated hydrocarbons (benzene, toluene, xylene etc.), arsenic, cadmium, uranium etc., can contaminate ground water (Garg, 2012).

In most cities and towns of India, the roads are littered with plastic bags and other wastes. The population explosion and rapid industrialization in India are leading to the migration of people from villages to cities. They generate thousands of tons of Municipal Solid Waste (MSW) daily. The amount of MSW shall increase significantly in the future as we are striving to become an industrialized country by the year 2020 (CPCB, 2004; Sharma and Shah, 2005). The poor waste collection and transportation facilities are accountable for the buildup of MSW at every nook and corner. The MSW management is at a critical stage due to lack of suitable facilities for treatment and its disposal. All the environmental components and human health are adversely affected due to unscientific disposal of MSW (Rathi, 2006; Ray etal;, 2005; Sharholy etal., 2008).The space requirement for dumping solid waste has become a severe problem in various cities all over the globe. Hence, the modern means of waste disposal, i.e. incineration and sanitary landfills, are now being used to resolve these problems. But, landfills and incineration of solid wastes are not satisfactory practices for waste disposal with respect to environment and human health. The integrated waste management plan for disposal of solid waste is the need of the hour for safeguarding biodiversity and environment. The waste collection, processing, resource recovery and the disposal should mesh with one another to achieve a common goal (Bharucha, 2004). The food habits, standard of living, commercial activities, and seasons are the factors affecting the quantity of MSW generated. Indian cities are now producing eight timesmore MSW as compared with that in 1947. The per capita MSW generation is expected to increase by 1-1.33% annually (Shekdar, 1999; Pappu etal., 2008). The per capita MSW generation in India range between 0.2 to 0.5 kg per day (Sharholy *et al.*, 2008).

MSW COMPOSITION

The composition and the amount of MSW produced decide the management system required to be planned, designed and operated. The solid wastes are classified in several ways. The classification is essential to tackle the complex problem of solid waste management in an efficient manner. The term solid waste usually represents most of the non-hazardous solid and semi-solid materials from a village, town, or city which requires regular collection and transport to a waste processing or final disposal site. The solid waste generated by domestic and commercial activities is classified as MSW, i.e. waste from homes, commercial establishments, institutions, and industrial facilities (Bharucha, 2004; Garg, 2012). However, it does not comprise wastes from construction and demolition, industrial processes, sewage sludge, mining, and agricultural wastes. MSW may contain a wide range of materials, i.e. food waste (vegetables, meat, egg shells, leftover food - wet garbage) as well as plastic, paper, tetra packs, newspaper, plastic cans, cardboard boxes, glass bottles, metal items, aluminum foil, wood pieces, etc. (dry garbage) and toxic substances (paints, pesticides, used batteries, medicines etc.) (Bharucha, 2004; Sharholy etal., 2008).The typical MSW composition (wet weight basis)in Indian cities, at source of generation and collection points, has been found to comprise primarily of a large fraction of organic matter (40-60%), fine earth and ash (30-40%), paper (3-6%), glass, plastic, and metals (each <1%). The C/N ratio varies between 20 to 30 with a lower calorific value range i.e. 800 and 1000 kcal per kg (Sharholy *et al.*, 2008).

MSW MANAGEMENT

The sustainable waste management can be achieved by adopting an integrated approach, i.e. avoiding waste generation, waste reduction, reuse, recycling, recovering, treatment and disposal. The waste management should be based on the 3R principles (Reduce, Reuse and Recycle) (Ministry of Environment and Forest, 2010). The integrated solid waste management (ISWM) involves technological, policy, administrative and legal actions to address the challenge of MSW management in the country. The ISWM involves managing waste in an environmentally sound, socially acceptable and techno-economically viable manner so as to effectively protect human health and biodiversity. ISWM involves evaluation of local needs and conditions for selecting and combining the most suitable waste management activities as per the conditions. The major activities involved under ISWM are waste prevention, recycling, composting, combustion, and final disposal in appropriately planned, constructed, and managed landfills. ISWM involves the selection and use of appropriate technologies and management programmes to accomplish specific waste management goals. The understanding of the interaction among different waste activities helps to prepare an ISWM plan in which the individual components complement each other (USEPA, 2004; Sridevi *et al.*, 2012).

Sustainable waste management can be attained by strategic planning, institutional capacity building, economically viable technologies, fiscal incentives, public-private and community participation etc. The waste collectors and recyclers should get technical and financial assistance in this endeavor. The cost sharing would increase viability and affordability of the waste management for regional landfill and waste treatment(Ministry of Environment and Forest, 2010). The MSW management involves activities associated with waste generation, storage, collection, transfer and transport, processing and disposal. But, in most cities, it involves only four steps i.e. waste generation, collection, transportation, and disposal (Bundela *et.al.*, 2010). The following approaches are part of an integrated sustainable waste management system.

WASTE REDUCTION AT SOURCE

The waste generation reduction at source is the best approach. We can use less material for manufacturing a product by on site reuse of product, improving product design or using less material for packaging. We should buy items with least packaging and avoid purchasing disposable items and also leave habit of asking for plastic bags (Bharucha, 2004). We should utilize reusable or recyclable products. Waste prevention is the highest priority in ISWM that seeks to decrease the quantity of waste which individuals, businesses and other institutions generate. By preventing waste generation, lesser effuse collection vehicles, smaller and fewer waste processing facilities would be needed. It would increase the life of landfills and the society would be benefited. There use of products and materials should be promoted after preventing waste generation. Reuse involves the recovery of materials to be used again, possibly after cleaning and refurbishing. Reuse of products conserves energy and water, decreases pollution, and conserves the natural resources as compared to the use of single-use products. Reuse of products is socially more desirable than recycling. Cardboard boxes can be folded and sent back to the company to be reused for shipping the same or other materials. Beverage bottles can be disposable, reusable or recyclable. Reusable bottle produce the least environmental impact, while the disposable one require the large energy, water and generate the huge quantity of waste and pollution (USEPA, 2004; Sridevi *et. al.*, 2012).

WASTE RECYCLING

Waste recycling means reuse of some of the components of MSW that have economic value. There are various benefits of recycling, i.e. resource conservation, reduction in energy and water requirement for manufacturing, and reduced pollution. Metals, paper, cardboard, ceramics, leather, rubber, wood, textiles, glass and plastic present in the MSW are recyclable materials. Aluminum and steel can be recycled several times. However, recycling also has several problems which are either technical or economical e.g. plastics are difficult to recycle due to use of different polymer resins for their manufacture. Hence, separation of different plastics prior to recycling is essential (Bharucha, 2004).The recyclable material varies from 13%-20%. Rag pickers play a key role in collection of the recyclable materials from the bins, roads and waste disposal sites. About 40% to 80% of plastic is recycled in India which is higher as compared with 10% to 15% of the developed nations. The recovery of paper has been 14% of the total consumption of paper in 1991.This is low as compared with the global recovery of 37% (CPCB, 2004; Pappu etal., 2008; khan 1994; Bhide and Shekdar, 1998). Recycling is a source of income to the scavengers who pick up recyclable materials. Factories that use recyclable materials as raw material can be built at a little cost as compared to the plants that use virgin materials. Recycling can help to maintain a competitive economy,clean environment, and achieve sustainable development. The government should recognize the social, economic and environmental impact of scavenging by legalizing it (USEPA, 2004; Sridevi etal., 2012).

WASTE DISPOSAL METHODS

1. Sanitary landfill

Open, poorly managed, and uncontrolled dumping of MSW is usually practiced in several cities. This practice has resulted in serious environmental degradation. Major part of MSW (>90%) in cities and towns is directly dumped on land in an unacceptable manner without following the principles of sanitary land filling. Sanitary land filling is a satisfactory and recommended technique for final disposal of MSW (Sharholy etal., 2008). But, the ISWM gives least priority to the final disposal of wastes at sanitary landfills. It is a facility designed particularly for the final disposal of wastes that reduces the risks to public health and the environment (Sridevi etal., 2012). The sanitary landfill is a depression in an impermeable soil layer that is lined with an impervious membrane. The waste is placed in a properly chosen landfill site in a carefully approved way. The solid waste is spread out and compacted using heavy machinery and is covered daily by a layer of compacted soil. The pollutants leaching out from the bottom of a landfill (leachates) often seep down to contaminate the groundwater aquifers. Hence, suitable bottom liners and leachate collection system should be used along with the regular monitoring system to detect pollution of groundwater.

The organic material of the buried waste is decomposed by the action of microorganisms. Initially, there will be aerobic decomposition of the waste as the oxygen is available in the fresh landfill. Later, the anaerobes take over by generating methane which is toxic and explosive when mixed with air (5-15%). The installation of a ventilation system to collect and vent blocked gas for safe dilution and dispersion into the atmosphere is essential part of the landfills design. But, the dumping sites are generally devoid of a leachate collection system or landfill gas monitoring and collection equipments (Bhide and Shekdar, 1998; Gupta *et al.*, 1998). Landfill is an economic alternative for MSW disposal but to find suitable landfill sites is becoming difficult. The availability of land for MSW disposal is a problem in cities like Delhi (Sharholy *et al.*, 2006). At the same time, there always remains the danger of environmental damage by leakage of leachates (Bharucha, 2004). The electricity may be produced by burning the methane collected from landfills. The landfills require considerable money and often face political obstacles for their building due to local resistance. The landfills are required for final waste disposal that could not be prevented, reused, recycled, or composted (Sridevi *et al.*, 2012).

2. Incineration

It is the process of burning MSW in an appropriately designed furnace at a suitable temperature (980-2000°C) for 1 hour. It is a chemical process where the combustible fraction of the waste is oxidized with oxygen producing carbon dioxide and water, which are dispersed into the atmosphere and heat is generated. Incineration results in about 90% and 75% reduction in volume and weight, respectively, of waste. It results in energy recovery and destruction of toxic wastes e.g. hospital waste (Bharucha, 2004;). The air quality, toxicity and disposal of the fly and bottom ash are the problems when the incineration is used as waste disposal method. There may be present heavy metals in incinerator ash which are harmful. Hence, materials containing heavy metals, e.g. batteries and plastics, should be segregated before incineration. The installation of air pollution control equipments and technical supervision by skilled employees are necessary (Bharucha, 2004). Incineration is not generally used in Indian cities because of the presence of high moisture (40-60%), organic waste (40-60%), inert material (30-50%), and low calorific value (800-1100 kcal per kg) in solid waste (Kansal, 2002; Gupta, 1998). The waste incineration occupies the next to last priority, after prevention, reuse, recycling and composting have been undertaken, in ISWM approach. The incineration experience in developing countries has been mostly negative due to high moisture content of the wastes (Sridevi etal., 2012).

3. Waste Derived Fuel

The biomass gasification and refuse derived fuel (RDF) are also the potential techniques available for MSW treatment. The burning of MSW in the absence of oxygen is known as waste gasification. The fuel gas is produced by gasification which is stored and used later. At present, few gasifiers are operational in India which are mostly being used for burning biomass i.e. agro-waste, forest wastes, and sawmill dust. This technology can be utilized for solid waste disposal after removal of moisture content and the inert materials, and reducing size of MSW by shredding. The waste is feed at a rate between50-150 kg per h and the efficiency achieved range between 70-80% [3, 20]. The RDF technology is aimed to manufacture improved solid fuel pellets from solid waste. The RDF pellets manufacture is about 210 t per day which is being used for power generation (~ 6.6 MW). Gasification–combustion and RDF seems to be promising technologies in terms of pollution reduction and power generation. They also help to reduce the pressure on landfills (Sharholy *et al.*, 2008).

4. Composting

The nature has perfect mechanisms for handling the waste. The biogeochemical cycles are instrumental in this respect to clear the wastes produced by plants and animals. We can mimic these natural processes (Bharucha, 2004). The conversion of the organic matter by bacteria, fungi, and worms, present in MSW, into compost (humus) in the presence of air under moist and hot conditions is known as composting. The compost has very high agricultural value and is applied as organic fertilizer in farms and gardens. It is non-odorous and free from pathogens (Ahsan, 1999). The microbes use the organic material as food and nutrients contained therein are ultimately returned to the soil to be used again by the organisms (Bharucha, 2004). The MSW volume can be decreased to 50-85% by the composting process. It maybe manual or mechanical process (Bhide and Shekdar, 1998). About 9% of MSW is treated by the composting process (Sharholy *et al.*, 2006). The efficiency of the composting is depends on various factors (Bernal *et al.*, 2008) various factors i.e. the formulation of the composting mix, pH, nutrient balance, particle size, porosity and moisture, O_2 concentration, temperature and water content. The composting takes place in two stages (Pereira, 1992). The initial, thermophilic, stage is characterized by increase in temperature (~ 65 °C) and the decomposition of readily degradable compounds i.e. sugars, fats, and proteins. The organic compounds are degraded to CO_2 and NH_3 with the utilization of O_2. The pH gets reduced due to formation of organic acids (Chen and Inbar, 1993). The pathogenic microorganisms are eliminated due to heat generation during thermophilic stage. Hence, the compost is safe to use by farmers. The second, stabilization, stage is characterized by reduction in temperature. The temperature remains between 25-30 °C and the humification of organic compost takes place. At the end, there occur increase in humic matter and cation exchange capacity (CEC) of the compost. The compost is a stabilized and sanitized end product of composting. The compost is beneficial for plant growth and is helpful for sustainable agriculture and resource management (Bernal, 2008; Pereia, 1992).

Vermi-composting utilizes the joint action of earthworms and aerobic microorganisms for stabilization of the organic matter. The biodegradable organic waste is initially decomposed by microbial action through extra cellular enzymes. The earthworms ingest the incompletely decayed matter and further decompose it in their gut into smaller sized particles. The worm casting is an odorless, fine, and granular material which is a bio-fertilizer. Vermi-composting requires larger area as compared with dry composting (Ghosh, 2004; Khan, 1994). When, the organic solid waste is buried in soil under partial anaerobic conditions, anaerobic microorganisms act upon it and release methane and carbon dioxide. The organic residue left after anaerobic decomposition is good compost. This process is known as bio-methanation. This is a slow process as compared to aerobic composting. This process leads to energy recovery in the form of biogas (55-60% methane) production which can be used for power generation. The controlled biomethanation process can produce 2-4 times more methane, in 3 weeks, from 1 t of MSW as will be produced in landfill in 6-7 years with same amount of MSW (Ahsan, 1999; Khan, 1994).

CONCLUSION

The people should be made aware about the health hazards of the wastes. The people and private sector active participation could improve the efficiency of MSW management. The MSW collection system should be strengthened and organized by regular collection of waste on specified timing. The waste segregation is the primary requirement for the scientific disposal of MSW. The recyclable material is a precious resource which should be recycled to derive the economic and environmental benefits. Resource recycling will help top grade technology, conserve resource, reduce landfill space need, and save energy. Composting is an ideal and popular MSW disposal method in India in place of incineration. But, it is a slow process and requires large land area. Sanitary land-filling should be limited to non-biodegradable and inert wastes that are not appropriate for composting or recycling (Sharholy *et al.*, 2008). MSW management in an environmentally sustainable manner is a challenge. This will require reuse and recycling of resource, waste to energy approach, and technology development for satisfactory waste disposal. The active participation of all the stakeholders, i.e. local government bodies, private entrepreneurs, non-government organizations, and civil society, is vital for the management of waste (Ministry of Environment and Forest, 2010).

REFERENCES

1. Ahsan, N., Solid Waste Management Plan for Indian Megacities, Indian Journal of Environmental Protection, 19 (2): 90-95 (1999).
2. Arau´jo, A.S.F., Santos, V.B., Monteiro, R.T.R., Responses of Soil Microbial Biomass and Activity for Practices of Organic and Conventional Farming Systems in Piauý´State, Brazil European Journal of Soil Biology, 44: 25-30 (2008).
3. Bernal, M.P., Albuquereque, J.A., Moral, R., Composting of Animal Manures and Chemical Criteria for Compost Maturity Assessment: A Review, Bioresource Technology, 99: 3372-3380 (2008).
4. Bharucha, E., Textbook for Environmental Studies for Undergraduate Courses of all Branches of Higher Education for University Grants Commission, New Delhi and Bharati Vidyapeeth Institute of Environment Education and Research, 145 (2004).
5. Bhide, A.D., Shekdar, A.V., Solid Waste Management in Indian Urban Centers, International Solid Waste Association Times (ISWA), (1): 26-28 (1998).
6. Bundela, P.S., Gautam, S.P., Pandey, A.K., Awasthi, M.K., Sarsaiya, S., Municipal Solid Waste Management in Indian Cities - A Review, International Journal of Environmental Sciences, 1 (4): (2010).
7. Central Pollution Control Board (CPCB), Management of Municipal Solid Waste, Ministry of Environment and Forests, New Delhi, India (2004).
8. Chen, Y., Inbar, U., Chemical and Spectroscopical Analyses of Organic Matter Transformation during Composting in Relation to Compost Maturity, In: Hoitink HAJ, Keener HM (eds), Science and Engineering of Composting: Design, Environmental, Microbiological and Utilization Aspects, Renaissance Publications, Worthington, OH, 550-600 (1993).
9. Garg, S.K., Environmental Engineering (Vol. II): Sewage Disposal and Air Pollution Engineering, Khanna Publishers, Daryaganj, New Delhi, 499 (2012).
10. Ghosh, C., Integrated Vermin - Pcsciculture - An Alternative Option for Recycling of Municipal Solid Waste in Rural India, Journal of Bioresource Technology, 93 (1): 71-75 2004.
11. Gupta, S., Krishna, M., Prasad, R.K., Gupta, S., Kansal, A., Solid Waste Management in India: Options and Opportunities. Resource, Conservation and Recycling, 24: 137-154 (1998).
12. Kansal, A., Solid Waste Management Strategies for India, Indian Journal of Environmental Protection, 22 (4): 444-448 (2002).

13. Khan, R.R., Environmental Management of Municipal Solid Wastes, Indian Journal of Environmental Protection, 14 (1): 26-30 (1994).

14. Ministry of Environment and Forests, Report of the Committee to Evolve Road Map on Management of Wastes in India, Final/09032010, MOEF, New Delhi, (March, 2010).

15. Pappu, A., Saxena, M., Asokar, S.R., Solid Waste Generation in India and Their Recycling Potential in Building Materials, Journal of Building and Environment, 42 (6): 2311-2324 (2007).

16. Pereira Neto, J.T., Stentiford, E.I., Aspectosepidemiolo´gicosdacompostagem, RevistaBiolo´gica, 27: 1-6 (1992).

17. Rathi, S., Alternative Approaches for Better Municipal Solid Waste Management in Mumbai, India, Journal of Waste Management, 26 (10): 1192-1200 (2006).

18. Ray, M.R., Roychoudhury, S., Mukherjee, G., Roy, S., Lahiri, T., Respiratory and General Health Impairments of Workers Wmployed in a Municipal Solid Waste Disposal at Open Landfill Site in Delhi, International Journal of Hygiene and Environmental Health, 108 (4): 255-262 (2005).

19. Sharholy, M., Ahmad, K., Mahmood, G., Trivedi, R.C., Development of Prediction Models for Municipal Solid Waste Generation for Delhi City, In: Proceedings of National Conference of Advanced in Mechanical Engineering (AIME-2006), Jamia Millia Islamia, New Delhi, India, 1176-1186 (2006).

20. Sharholy, M., Ahmad, K., Mahmood, G., Trivedi, R.C., Municipal Solid Waste Management in Indian Cities - A Review, Waste Management, (28): 459-467 (2008).

21. Sharma, S., Shah, K.W., Generation and Disposal of Solid Waste in Hoshangabad, In: Book of Proceedings of the Second International Congress of Chemistry and Environment, Indore, India, 749-751 (2005).

22. Shekdar, A.V., Municipal Solid Waste Management - The Indian Perspective, Journal of Indian Association for Environmental Management, 26 (2): 100-108 (1999).

23. Sridevi, V., Modi, M., Lakshmi, M.V.V.C., kesavarao, L., A Review on Integrated Solid Waste Management, International Journal of Engineering Science and Advanced Technology, 2 (5): 1491-1499 (2012).

24. United States Environmental Protection Agency, EPA530-F-02-026a (5306W).

25. Yelda, S., Kansal, S., Economic Insight into MSWM in Mumbai: A Critical Analysis, International Journal of Environmental Pollution, 19 (5): 516-527 (2003).

Pages: 37-56

WASTE MANAGEMENT AND ENVIRONMENTAL HEALTH

Edited by: **Dr. B. Tabassum; Dr. Priya Bajaj & Dr. Pawan Kumar 'Bharti'**

ISBN: 978-93-5056-777-7

Edition: **2016**

Published by: **Discovery Publishing House Pvt. Ltd., New Delhi (India)**

Present Scenario of Obsolete Pesticides on Public Health and Environment

Virendra Kumar[1] and **Chandrika Chaurasia**[2]

ABSTRACT

Pesticides have been used worldwide as a mean to increase agricultural output, fight pests and control tropical diseases. Thousands of active chemical ingredients have been in use to that aim, some of them proving to be highly efficient and therefore popular like *DDT* or *endosulfan*. However, with increasing and prolonged use, also negative impacts

[1]Plant Protection Officer (Plant Pathology), Regional Pesticides Testing Laboratory, Ministry of Agriculture, Department of Agriculture and Co-operation, Directorate of Plant Protection, Quarantine and Storage, Govt. of India, Email: drkumarvirendra@gmail.com

[2]Department of Chemistry, Govt. Raza P.G. College, Rampur, 244 901, (U.P.).

Email: chandrikachaurasia25@gmail.com

Corresponding Author: Dr. Virendra Kumar, Plant Protection Officer (Plant Pathology), Regional Pesticides Testing Laboratory, T-2, Ratan Lal Nagar, Kanpur, U.P.

Email: drkumarvirendra@gmail.com *Mob.*: +91 - 9415695944

became noticeable such as an increase of disease rates, infertility and sometimes death, or environmental impacts including contamination of local water supplies, global transport and bio-accumulation of persistent organic pollutants (POPs), or loss of income to farmers whose products contains unacceptable concentrations of pesticide residues to be fit for sale. An additional problem is the build-up of large stocks of obsolete pesticides (OPs) over time, stemming from overuse and mismanagement of pesticides or because stocks became unusable due to long-term storage leading to degradation. Today, there is an estimated global challenge of 5-10 million tons of obsolete pesticides and related production wastes which needs to be addressed to reduce risks to public health or the environment. Due to the more lethal effects few pesticides are totally ban to use in the India.

Keywords: Obsolete pesticides (OPs), Persistent organic pollutants (POPs), Public health & Bio-accumulation.

INTRODUCTION

Pesticide use is an integral part of our modern society, whether we consider the developed or the developing nations and their impact on human health is an important research subject. Most of developing countries have outdated and deteriorated stocks of pesticides up to half of million tons of obsolete pesticides are scattered throughout the developing world. These toxic chemicals, often stored in leaking containers are seeping into soil and water. These stocks are often stored in poor conditions and pose a threat to human health and the environment. With the exception of a few newly industrialized countries, developing countries do not have adequate facilities to dispose of such stocks in a safe and environmentally sound manner. In many cases, therefore, the recommended disposal method would appear to be shipment of the pesticides to a country that has special hazardous waste incineration facilities.

In view of the dangerous nature of these pesticides and the high costs of safe and environmentally sound disposal, the long-term solution to obsolete stocks lies in preventive measures: improved stock management and reduction of stocks.

The objective of these guidelines is to raise awareness about the mechanisms through which obsolete pesticide stocks accumulate and to enhance the formulation of policies and procedures aimed at prevention of such accumulation. The guidelines analyze the causes of this accumulation and recommend how it can be prevented. They provide guidance to the governments of developing countries, aid agencies and the pesticide industry. For developing countries, they are considered of special interest to ministries of agriculture and ministries of health, particularly for senior staff responsible for assessing the country's yearly pesticide requirements and for procuring pesticides; staff responsible for the management of national pesticide stocks; heads of departments or services responsible for plant protection, migratory pest control and vector control; directors of produce boards and cooperatives involved in large-scale pesticide distribution; and others responsible for pesticide procurement and management.

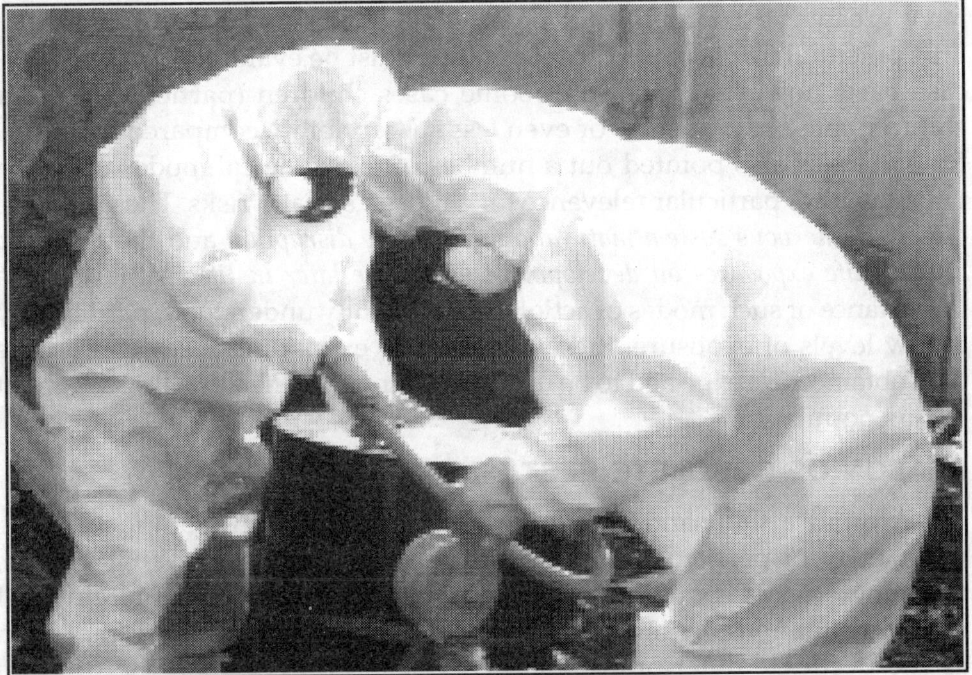

Fig. 4.1: **Handling of Obsolete Pesticides**

The guidelines should be regarded as a further instrument to enhance implementation of the FAO *International Code of Conduct on the Distribution and Use of Pesticides*, which was adopted by the Conference of FAO in 1985. The objective of the Code of Conduct is to set forth responsibilities and establish voluntary standards of conduct for all public and private entities engaged in or affecting the distribution and use of pesticides, particularly where there is either an inadequate national law or no law regulating pesticides. The Code of Conduct was amended in 1989 to include the Prior Informed Consent (PIC) procedure (FAO, 1990).

The guidelines supplement the *Guidelines on disposal of bulk quantities of pesticides in developing countries*. The issue of obsolete pesticide stocks is increasingly receiving international attention. A growing number of developing countries are requesting aid agencies to provide assistance for disposal of obsolete stocks and this has already started, together with assistance aimed at preventing further accumulation of obsolete pesticide stocks.

Infants and young children constitute a particular population of concern in terms of exposure to pesticides (including obsolete pesticides). For various reasons (behavioral, anatomical and metabolic) children may have greater susceptibility to the adverse effects of pesticide exposure. This potential for increased susceptibility must be evaluated on a case-by-case basis however, because in some cases children (particularly older children) may have similar or even less susceptibility compared to adults. Research has also pointed out a number of toxicological modes of action that may be of particular relevance for children's health risks. These include effects on *nervous system maturation*, *endocrine disruption* and the *influence of early life exposures on development of disease later in life*. Although the importance of such modes of action is not yet fully understood, particularly at low levels of exposure, these are areas of expanding research and the data obtained are expected to be useful for improving health risk assessment in this population.

REASON OF OBSOLETE PESTICIDE

Around a thousand active ingredient are used to manufacture the wide array of pesticides in countries all over the world. What's more, these ingredients come in many thousands of different formulations. All these formulations degrade over time. The chemical by-products that form as the pesticide deteriorates can be even more toxic than the original product. Obsolete pesticide stocks piles are often poorly stored and the containers corrode and leak. In a single stored facility, chemicals from many different products may blend together to create a toxic quagmire. Because of this tremendous chemical complexity, there is no single solution that can be applied to clean up obsolete pesticide stocks. The only way can permanently eliminate the dangers posed by old and unwanted pesticide stocks are to make sure that no more stocks accumulate. That's why it is essential to understand the reasons behind the build-up of existing obsolete pesticides stockpiles. As the philosopher *George Santayana* said,

"Those who cannot learn from history are doomed to repeat it"

The major factors that have resulted in the creation of large quantities of old and unused pesticides in environment are:

(i) Banned pesticides

In many countries, when a range of products has been banned or withdrawn for health or environmental reasons stocks remain where they are stored and eventually deteriorate. Good practice in such cases requires pesticides regulatory authorities to allow so that existing stocks can be used up before the restriction is fully applied. Some 25 pesticides are banned for manufacture, import and use in India. Two other pesticides and formulations are banned for use in the country but their manufacture is allowed for export, it has been revealed under the Right to Information (RTI) Act. Large bird kills, especially of Swainson's Hawks from the prairies and grasslands of western North America, have been reported allegedly from the use of monocrotophos. On the 'banned' pesticides and formulations list are aldrin, Benzene hexachloride, Calcium cyanide, Chlordane, Copper cetoarsenite, Cibromochloropropane, Endrin, Ethel mercury chloride, Ethyl parathion, Heptachlor, Menzaone, Nitrofen, Paraquat dimethyl suplhate, Pentachlorophenol, Phenyl mercury acetate, Sodium methane arsonate, Tetradifon, Toxafen, aldicarb, Chlorobenzilate, Dieldrine, Maleic hydrazide, Ethylene dibromide, and TCA (trichloro acetic acid). India has currently banned for use two pesticides and formulations - the suspected neurotoxicant nicotin sulfate and the Bangalore-manufactured broad-spectrum protective contact fungicide captafol 80 per cent powder - but their manufacture is allowed for export. In the 17th century, nicotine sulfate was extracted from tobacco leaves for use as an insecticide. The 19th century saw the introduction of two more natural pesticides, *Pyrethrum*, which is derived from *Chrysanthemums*, and *Rotenone*, derived from the roots of tropical vegetables. In 1939, Paul Müller discovered that DDT was a very effective insecticide. By the 1960s, DDT was found to be preventing many fish-eating birds from reproducing, threatening biodiversity. DDT is now banned in at least 86 countries, but it is still used in parts of the world, seen as needed to prevent malaria and other tropical diseases by killing mosquitoes and other disease-carrying insects. Currently, *India has 238 pesticides registered under Section 9(3) of the Insecticide Act 1968*.

(ii) The ban on persistent organic pollutants (POPs)

As the world become more aware of the dangers of POPs chemicals, these pesticides were banned from donor-funded campaigns in the late 1970s. Many POPs pesticides, dieldrin in particular, were widely used in campaigns to eradicate locusts in Africa. When the POPs pesticides were banned, little thought was given to the fate of the remaining stock. Existing data indicate that more than 20 per cent of obsolete pesticides stockpiles consist of POP pesticides which are nearly 30 years old. They are poorly stored and are leaking into the environment and contaminating soil and water. Also, because they are very persistent, POPs pesticides can be effective for a long time. As results, the pesticides are sometimes stolen and sold illegally.

Table 4.1: List of Banned, Pesticides. (As on 01st January 2014 by Central Insecticide Board (CIB) and Registration Committee (RC), Faridabad)

Category	Sl. No.	Pesticides/Formulations Banned in India
A. Pesticides Banned for manufacture, import and use	1.	Aldicarb
	2.	Aldrin
	3.	Benzene Hexachloride
	4.	Calcium Cyanide
	5.	Chlorbenzilate
	6.	Chlordane
	7.	Chlorofenvinphos
	8.	Copper Acetoarsenite
	9.	Dibromochloropropane
	10.	Dieldrin
	11.	Endrin
	12.	Ethyl Mercury Chloride
	13.	Ethyl Parathion
	14.	Ethylene Dibromide
	15.	Heptachlor
	16.	Lindane (Gamma-HCH)

(Contd…)

Category	Sl. No.	Pesticides/Formulations Banned in India
	17.	Maleic Hydrazide
	18.	Menazon
	19.	Metoxuron
	20.	Nitrofen
	21.	Paraquat Dimethyl Sulphate
	22.	Pentachloro Nitrobenzene
	23.	Pentachlorophenol
	24.	Phenyl Mercury Acetate
	25.	Sodium Methane Arsonate
	26.	TCA (Trichloro acetic acid)
	27.	Tetradifon
	28.	Toxaphene (Camphechlor)
B. Pesticide formulations banned for import, manufacture and use	1.	Carbofuron 50% SP
	2.	Methomyl 12.5% L
	3.	Methomyl 24% formulation
	4.	Phosphamidon 85% SL
C. Pesticide/Pesticide formulations banned for use but continued to manufacture for export	1.	Captafol 80% Powder
	2.	Nicotin Sulfate
D. Pesticides Withdrawn*	1.	Dalapon
	2.	Ferbam
	3.	Formothion
	4.	Nickel Chloride
	5.	Paradichlorobenzene (PDCB)
	6.	Simazine
	7.	Warfarin

* Withdrawal may become inoperative as soon as required complete data as per the guidelines is generated and submitted by the Pesticides Industry to the Government and accepted by the Registration Committee. S.O 915(E) dated 15th Jun,2006

Table 4.2: List of Refused Registration Pesticides. (As on 01st January 2014 by Central Insecticide Board (CIB) and Registration Committee (RC), Faridabad)

Sl. No.	Pesticides Refused Registration
1.	Ammonium Sulphamate
2.	Azinphos Ethyl
3.	Azinphos Methyl
4.	Binapacryl
5.	Calcium Arsenate
6.	Carbophenothion
7.	Chinomethionate (Morestan)
8.	Dicrotophos
9.	EPN
10.	Fentin Acetate
11.	Fentin Hydroxide
12.	Lead Arsenate
13.	Leptophos (Phosvel)
14.	Mephosfolan
15.	Mevinphos (Phosdrin)
16.	2,4, 5-T
17.	Thiodemeton/Disulfoton
18.	Vamidothion

There are many cases where highly hazardous pesticides, which are not permitted for use in industrialized countries, are exported to developing countries. For a pesticide to be banned, it has to be registered first. Some pesticides companies have not registered or re-registered products which they knew would have not been authorized in their own country but continue to produce and export the same products to developing countries. There are also cases of Pesticides manufactures increasing export of products that have been banned or restricted in their own countries, possibly in order to use up existing stocks or to compensate for depleted local markets.

Table 4.3: List of Pesticides Restricted for Use in India. (As on 01st January 2014 by Central Insecticide Board (CIB) and Registration Committee (RC), Faridabad)

Sl. No.	Pesticides Restricted for Use	Details of Restrictions
1.	Aluminium Phosphide	• The Pest Control Operations with Aluminium Phosphide may be undertaken only by Govt./Govt. undertakings/Govt. Organizations/pest control operators under the strict supervision of Govt. Experts or experts whose expertise is approved by the Plant Protection Advisor to Govt. of India except [1]Aluminium Phosphide 15 % 12 g tablet and [2]Aluminum Phosphide 6 % tablet. • The production, marketing and use of Aluminium Phosphide tube packs with a capacity of 10 and 20 tablets of 3 g each of Aluminium Phosphide are banned completely. (S.O.677 (E) dated 17thJuly, 2001)
2.	Captafol	• The use of Captafol as foliar spray is banned. Captafol shall be used only as seed dresser. (S.O.569 (E) dated 25thJuly, 1989). • The manufacture of Captafol 80 % powder for dry seed treatment (DS) is banned for use in the country except manufacture for export. (S.O.679 (E) dated 17thJuly, 2001)
3.	Cypermethrin	• Cypermethrin 3% Smoke Generator is to be used only through Pest Control Operators and not allowed to be used by the General Public. [Order of Hon' ble High Court of Delhi in WP(C) 10052 of 2009 dated 14-07-2009 and LPA-429/ 2009 dated 08-09-2009].
4.	Dazomet	• The use of Dazomet is not permitted on Tea. (S.O.3006 (E) dated 31st Dec, 2008)
5.	Diazinon	• Diazinon is banned for use in agriculture except for household use. (S.O.45 (E) dated 08th Jan, 2008)

(Contd...)

Sl. No.	Pesticides Restricted for Use	Details of Restrictions
6.	Dichloro Diphenyl Trichloroethane (DDT)	• The use of DDT for the domestic Public Health Programme is restricted up to 10,000 Metric Tonnes per annum, except in case of any major outbreak of epidemic. M/s Hindustan Insecticides Ltd.,the sole manufacturer of DDT in the country may manufacture DDT for export to other countries for use in vector control for public health purpose. The export of DDT to Parties and State non-Parties shall be strictly in accordance with the paragraph 2(b) article 3 of the Stockholm Convention on Persistent Organic Pollutants (POPs). (S.O.295 (E) dated 8th March, 2006) • Use of DDT in Agriculture is withdrawn. In very special circumstances warranting the use of DDT for plant protection work, the state or central Govt. may purchase it directly from M/s Hindustan Insecticides Ltd. to be used under expert Governmental supervision. (S.O.378 (E) dated 26thMay, 1989)
7.	Fenitrothion	• The use of Fenitrothion is banned in Agriculture except for locust control in scheduled desert area and public health. (S.O.706 (E) dated 03rdMay, 2007)
8.	Fenthion	• The use of Fenthion is banned in Agriculture except for locust control, household and public health.(S.O.46 (E) dated 08th Jan, 2008)
9.	Methoxy Ethyl Mercuric Chloride (MEMC)	• The use of MEMC is banned completely except for seed treatment of potato and sugarcane. (S.O. 681 (E) dated 17th July, 2001)
10.	Methyl Bromide	• Methyl Bromide may be used only by Govt./Govt. undertakings/Govt. Organizations/Pest control operators under the strict supervision of Govt. Experts or Experts whose expertise is approved by the Plant Protection Advisor to Govt. of India. [G.S.R.371 (E) dated 20thMay, 1999 and earlier RC decision]

(Contd...)

Sl. No.	Pesticides Restricted for Use	Details of Restrictions
11.	Methyl Parathion	• Methyl Parathion 50 % EC and 2% DP formulations are banned for use on fruits and vegetables. (S.O.680 (E) dated 17th July, 2001) • The use of Methyl Parathion is permitted only on those crops approved by the Registration Committee where honeybees are not acting as pollinators. (S.O.658 (E) dated 04th Sep., 1992.)
12.	Monocrotophos	• Monocrotophos is banned for use on vegetables. (S.O.1482 (E) dated 10th Oct, 2005)
13.	Sodium Cyanide	• The use of Sodium Cyanide shall be restricted for Fumigation of Cotton bales under expert supervision approved by the Plant Protection Advisor to Govt. of India. (S.O.569(E) dated 25th July, 1989)

Authorities within the country must identify the root cause for the accumulation of the stocks and adopt measures to ensure that no more stocks will accumulate. By following the *International Code of Conduct on the Distribution and Use of Pesticides*, government can ensure that useless or unwanted pesticides don't enter the country and that the pesticides that are allowed in are stored and managed safety. The FAO Programme on *Prevention and Disposal of Obsolete Pesticides* has published several guidelines specifically related to the prevention of obsolete stocks.

FAOs programme on the prevention and disposal of obsolete pesticides assists developing countries deals with these toxic containers.

- FAO Pesticide disposal series 14: The preparation of inventories of Pesticides and contaminated materials.
- FAO Pesticide disposal series 15: Environmental management Tool kit for obsolete pesticide (EMTK).
- FAO Pesticides Disposal Series 16: Environmental management Tool Kit for obsolete pesticide (EMTK)

Often stockpiles old pesticides are poorly stored and toxic chemicals leak into the environment, turning potentially fertile soil into hazardous waste the programme also provides strategies for handling contaminated soil.

CONTAINERS OF PESTICIDE

Wherever pesticides are used, empty containers are generated. Obviously, no country can eliminate the problem of used pesticide containers in a single, or even a series, of disposal operations. It's an ongoing problem; empty pesticides containers are highly valued property, even though it is usually impossible to remove all traces of toxic chemicals from pesticides containers, people often use them for storing fuel or even food and water. This is clearly unsafe practice that must be discouraged. When measures are taken to dispose of containers, often they are not appropriate. For example, many pesticides suppliers and national authorities recommend the burying or burning of waste pesticides and empty containers. But buried chemical waste can contaminate soil and ground water, while burning pesticides and containers releases highly toxic fumes. Often pesticides, empty containers and contaminated materials are dumped in landfills or other general waste collection sites. Most of these sites aren't designated to prevent toxic materials from leaking into the ground or being washed out by rain water bodies. In developing countries such sites are also usually scavenged and useful items such as pesticide containers are reclaimed.

PROBLEMS IN CLEANING OF OBSLETE PESTICIDES

Disposal of obsolete pesticides currently cost between 3 and 5 USD per kilogram or liter of pesticide or contaminated material. This covers the cost of repacking, site clean-up, overland transportation, shipment to Europe and incineration in dedicated high-temperature hazardous waste incinerators. To date about 3000 tons of obsolete pesticides have been disposed of from 14 countries at a cost of almost 14 million. On the basis of global estimate totaling 250 000 tons of obsolete pesticides, about 1.25 billion would be needed to destroy all the stock.

GOVERNMENT AGENCIES INVOLVED IN REGULATION OF OBSOLETE PESTICIDES

Various government agencies are involved in the regulation of the pesticide industry in India. The Ministry of Agriculture regulates the manufacture, sale, transport and distribution, export, import and use of pesticides through the 'Insecticides Act 1968' and the rules framed there under. The Central Insecticides Board (CIB), advises the Central and state governments on technical matters. The approval of the use of pesticides and new formulations to tackle the pest problem in various crops is given by the Registration Committee (RC) while the Union Ministry of Health and Family Welfare monitors and regulates pesticides residue levels in food. It also sets maximum residue limits (MRL) of pesticides on food commodities. In India, the pesticides regulations are governed under the following Acts/Rules:

1. The Insecticides Act 1968 and Rules 1971.
2. Prevention of Food Adulteration Act 1954.
3. The Environment (Protection) Act 1986.
4. The Factories Act 1948.
5. Bureau of Indian Standards Act.
6. Air (Prevention & Control of Pollution) Act 1981.
7. Water (Prevention & Control of Pollution) Act 1974.
8. Hazardous Waste (Management & Handling) Rules 1989.

Following ministries are involved in the regulation of the pesticide industry in India:

1. The ministry of Agriculture.
2. The Union Ministry of Health and Family.
3. The Ministry of Environment, Forest and Climate change.
4. The Ministry of Consumers Affairs, Food and Public Distribution.

Following government agencies are involved in the regulation of the pesticide applications in India:

1. The central insecticide board (CIB).
2. Registration Committee (RC).
3. Bureau of Indian Standards (BIS).

SAFE AND JUDICIOUS USE OF PESTICIDES

Judicious use of pesticide is the need based correct use of appropriate pesticide in an ecologically compatible manner so as to reap maximum benefits by achieving cost effective pest management without harming environment and non-target species.

Fig. 4.2: **Safe Use of Pesticides**

Table 4.4: List of Do's and Don'ts During Use of Pesticides

Sl. No.	Works Performed at the Time of	Do's	Don'ts
1.	Purchase	Purchase only required quantity	• Do not purchase leaking containers, loose, unsealed ot torn bags • Do not purchase without proper/approved label.
2.	Storage	• Avoid storage in the house premises. • Store only in origional container with intact seal. • Keep away from reach of children and livestock.	• Do not expose to sunlight or rain water. • Do not store herbicide with other insecticide
3.	Handling	• Avoid carrying bulk on head, shoulders or on back.	• Never carry/transport pesticides along with food materials.
4.	Preparation of spray solution	• Use clean water. • Protect nose, eye, mouth, ears and hands. • Read the lebel before preparing. • Prepare as per recommendation only. • Add pesticides while agitating the water.	• Pesticides should not come in the direct contact on skin or on hands. • Do not smell the pesticides. • Do not eat, drink, smoke or chew while preparing solution.
5.	Equipment	• Select right kind of equipment. • Select right kind of Nozzle.	• Do not use leaky, defective equipment. • Do not blow/clean clogged nozzles with mouth.
6.	Spraying	• Apply only at recommended dose and dilution.	• Do not apply on hot sunny days and strong windy conditions. • Do not apply when rain is predicted or immediately after rain. • Do not apply against the wind direction.

(Contd...)

Sl. No.	Works Performed at the Time of	Do's	Don'ts
7.	Disposal	• Left over spray solutions should not be drained in pounds or water lines. • Throught it in barren, isolated area. • Used/empty containers should be crushed with a stone or stick. • Bured deep in to soil away from the source.	• Never reuse pesticide container for any purpose.
8.	Wash the sprayer or bucket with soap water after use.	• Avoid entry of workers and animal immediately after spraying.	• Do not use the same container for domestic purposes.
9.	Seed treatment	• Use metal seed dresser, earthen pots or polythene bags.	• Do not open lid or cover immediately after treatment. • Do not use left over seeds for human consumption or animal feed. • Do not use bare hands during seedling root dips.
10.	Harvest	• Observed safety interval	• Do not harvest immediately after applications. • Do not spray/dip harvest fruits in pesticides.

Warning Symbol of Pesticides Application

The following pictures showing the warning symbol of pesticides if we observed the following symbol on the packets/cans etc, then we can avoid the contact from that particular organisms.*

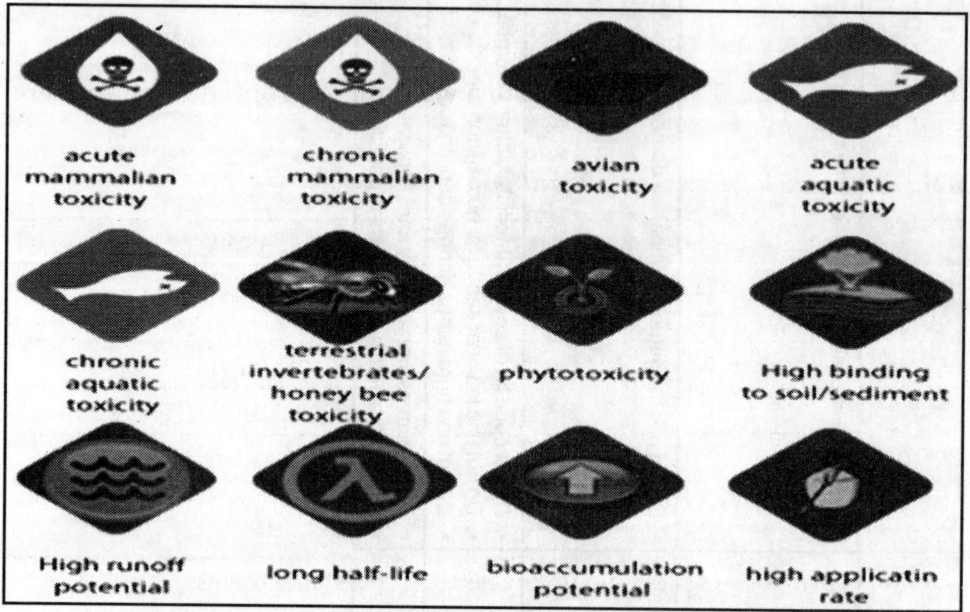

Fig. 4.3: **Various Types of Warning Symbol of Pesticides**

First Aids and Antidotes of Pesticides Poisoning

Procedures for first aid vary according to the type of exposure. In all cases, a person with knowledge of the incident should accompany the victim to the medical facility to inform qualified medical personnel about the nature of accident, the material being used, the first aid given and the victim's symptoms following exposure up to the time of his arrival at the medical facility.

- **Pesticides on skin:** Remove contaminated clothing and shoes. Wash skin and hairs with soap and plenty of water. Call a physician.
- **Pesticides in eyes:** Flush the eyes with running water for for 15 minutes. Use a low-pressure water source. Call a physician.
- **Pesticides inhaled:** Remove victim to fresh air and have him lie down. Loosen his clothing and keep him warm and quite. Apply mouth to mouth resuscitation if breathing stops. Apply cardiopulmonary resuscitation if breathing and heart beat stops. Get medical help immediately.

- **Pesticides swallowed:** Induce vomiting only if specified on the pesticide label. Apply cardiopulmonary resuscitation if breathing and heart beat stops. Get medical help immediately.

ANTIDOTE

An antidote is a substance which can counteract a form poisoning. Some of the more common pesticides and the appropriate antidote are listed in table 4.5.

Table 4.5: Antidotes of Some Common Pesticides

Antidote or Treatment	Group
Atropine with 2- PAM in symtomatic dosage artificial respiration may be required	Organo phosphates
Atropine, artificial respiration may be necessary	Carbamates
Barbiturates if convulsions occur	Chlorinated Hydrocarbon
Promotion	Botanicals
Intravenous sodium nitrite followed by Sodium thiosulfate	Fumigants
Intravenous barbiturates and procaine amide Soluble Vitamin K	Rodenticides

MANAGEMENT OF OBSOLETE PESTICIDES

The FAO Programme cannot do its work without donor support.

The Netherlands has been a key supporter in matters relating to obsolete pesticides. It has funded the FAO obsolete pesticides programme since its inception in 1994.

It has also funded several national disposal programmes including those in Ethiopia, Seychelles, the United Republic of Tanzania and Zanzibar, Yemen, and Zambia. The Netherlands also funded a detailed inventory of stocks in the United Republic of Tanzania and Pakistan.

Other countries that have funded obsolete pesticide disposal projects in collaboration with FAO are: Belgium, Finland, Japan, Sweden and United States of America.

Rachel Carson's passionate warning in the seminal 1962 book *'Silent Spring'*, which is now celebrating 53 years from its publication, concern on the steadily increasing accumulation in the environment of chemically robust, biologically persistent and possibly toxic organo-chlorine pesticides led to their substitution with less threatening products and finally to stop or limit their production and to severely restrict their use. In particular, the Stockholm Convention on Persistent Organic Pollutants (POPS) signed in 2001 banned or greatly restricted 12 chlorinated organic compounds or classes due to their toxicity and ability to accumulate in the environment and to magnify through the global trophic network. Among them are 11 pesticides namely *aldrin, chlordane, DDT, dieldrin, endrin, heptachlor, hexachloro-benzene, kepone, lindane, mirex,* and *toxaphene.* These pesticides played a historical role in mitigating the health impact of parasite-borne human pathogens such as malaria parasites and in protecting food crops to allow better feeding of an increasingly raising population especially in sub-tropical and tropical areas. Concern for human and environmental health is mainly due to long-term effects of some substances, in particular through endocrine disruption, interference with reproduction, carcinogenicity, although the actual size of effects of real-life exposure is still an active and debated research topic. Risk assessment and risk-benefit analysis of some key pesticides such as DDT still need a thorough understanding of the toxicity mechanisms and of its relevance to humans in the different life-stages.

As a consequence of the Stockholm ban, large stockpiles of unusable pesticides accumulate in some countries and thus present considerable threat to the environment and to human health, also due to unavoidable degradation of the active formulated substances into poorly tractable materials. To avoid environmental damage through contamination of water and agricultural land resources by leaching or improper disposal of repositories, inventories of existing stockpiles are needed to plan and carry adequately safe disposal interventions. Methods for disposal need to tackle the peculiar chemical characteristics of these highly chlorinated aliphatic and aromatic compounds, *i.e.,* very low water solubility and an unusual stability towards acid, basic and oxidizing conditions. Research and technology development in this field is currently exploiting the most advanced 'green chemistry' approaches, aimed at an as complete mineralization of organochlorine substrates with as negligible production of toxic waste. The government and concerned agencies should take out the initiatives to quick and safe disposal of obsolete pesticides and also take care that no new stock will be accumulated in the future. The obsolete pesticides may cause health risks such as, *headache, vomiting, heart complaint, foul smell, unconsciousness, drowsiness, irritation, eye problem, skin problem,* and *loss of concentration* etc.

Pesticide residues, some of which even belong to POPs category, in the soil near the warehouse were found having adverse impacts on the human health and environment of the study area. The constant presence of such pesticides over a long time or even increasing level of some obsolete pesticides in the soil confirmed that the pesticides had persistence nature and their concentrations in the soil was increasing with time along with the potential of increasing health hazards. Government needs to pay special attention towards the safer disposal of obsolete pesticides to protect the environment and public health and to ensure clean and healthy environment, which is the basic right of the citizen and the state is responsible to guarantee it.

REFERENCES

1. Environmental Security Assessment and Management of Obsolete Pesticides in Southeast Europe, NATO Science for Peace and Security Series C: Environmental Security 2013, pp. 301-309.
2. Environmental Security Assessment and Management of Obsolete Pesticides in Southeast Europe, NATO Science for Peace and Security Series C: Environmental Security 2013, pp. 139-145.
3. Gupta, P.K., 2004. Pesticide Exposure-Indian Scene, Toxicology, 198: 83-90.
4. http://www.google.co.in/imgres?imgurl=http://sccoastalpesticides.org/images/warning_symbols.png&imgrefurl.
5. https://www.dnb.co.in/Chemical_2010/pestiChapter3.asp
6. https://www.google.co.in/search?q=Warning+sign+of+pesticides&sa=X&biw=1024&bih=677&tbm=isch&imgil.
7. Journalist, Pesticides Watch Kathamadnu, Nepal, pp. 24-25.
8. Kandel, K.R. and Mainali, M., 1993. Playing with Poison. The Nepal Forum of Environment.
9. Lecture Notes on Pesticides Managements (2013) Obsolete Pesticides, National Institute of Plant Health Managements (NIPHM, Hyderabad), Page No. 44-46.
10. Manandhar, D.N., 2006. Pesticides Use in Nepal.
11. MOEST, 2005. Inventory of Pesticides in Nepal. POPs Enabling Activities Project, MOEST, Nepal.
12. MOEST, 2007. National Implementation Plan for The Stockholm Convention on Persistent Organic, Pollutants. POPs Enabling Activities Project, MOEST, Nepal.
13. Pimentel, D., 1992. Environment and Human Cost of Pesticides Use. Bioscience, 42: 740-760.
14. Pimentel, D.L. and McLaughlen. 1991. Environmental and Economic Impacts of Reducing U.S. Agricultural Pesticide use. In: D.Pimentel and A.A. Hanson (Eds.) CRC Handbook of Pest Management in Agriculture. 2nd ed. Vol. I. CRC Press. Boca Raton, pp. 679-718.
15. Thomas A. Lewandowski (2013) Factors Influencing Pesticide Risks for Children, NATO Science for Peace and Security Series C: Environmental Security 2013, pp. 185-200.

16. World Health Organization (1990): Public Health Impact of Pesticides Used in Agriculture, WHO, Geneva.
17. WWF, 1995. Environmental Impact from Nepal's Use of Chemical Pesticides. World Wildlife Fund.
18. WWF, 2005. Toxic Fact Sheet, World Wildlife Fund http://www.worldwildlife.org/toxics/pubs.cfm

***Pages:* 57-61**

WASTE MANAGEMENT AND ENVIRONMENTAL HEALTH

***Edited by:* Dr. B. Tabassum; Dr. Priya Bajaj & Dr. Pawan Kumar 'Bharti'**

ISBN: 978-93-5056-777-7

***Edition:* 2016**

***Published by:* Discovery Publishing House Pvt. Ltd., New Delhi (India)**

Microalgae and Wastewater Treatment

Alina Javed* and **Priya Bajaj****

ABSTRACT

Organic and inorganic substances which are released into the environment as a result of domestic, agricultural and industrial water activities lead to organic and inorganic pollution. The normal primary and secondary treatment processes of these wastewaters have been introduced in a growing number of places, in order to eliminate the easily settled materials and to oxidize the organic material present in wastewater. The result is a clear, apparently clean effluent which is discharged into natural water bodies. This secondary effluent is, however, loaded with inorganic nitrogen and phosphorus and causes

*Department of Biotechnology, Jamia Millia Islamia, New Delhi.

**Department of Zoology, Govt. Raza PG College, Rampur (UP) Email: alina.ally1@gmail.com

Corresponding Author: Alina Javed, Azad Colony, Infront of Ahteram Medical Store, Saharanpur (UP)

E-mail: alina.ally1@gmail.com, *Mob.* : +917417699239

eutrophication and more long-term problems because of refractory organics and heavy metals that are discharged. Microalgae culture offers an interesting step for wastewater treatments, because they provide a tertiary bio-treatment coupled with the production of potentially valuable biomass, which can be used for several purposes. Microalgae cultures offer an elegant solution to tertiary and quandary treatments due to the ability of microalgae to use inorganic nitrogen and phosphorus for their growth. And also, for their capacity to remove heavy metals, as well as some toxic organic compounds, therefore, it does not lead to secondary pollution. In the current review we will highlight on the role of microalgae in the treatment of wastewater.

INTRODUCTION

Pollution is a man-made phenomenon, arising either when the concentrations of naturally occurring substances are increased or when non-natural synthetic compounds (xenobiotics) are released into the environment. Organic and inorganic substances which are released into the environment as a result of domestic, agricultural and industrial water activities lead to organic and inorganic pollution. One of the major sources of water pollution is the uncontrolled discharge of human wastes, inappropriate sanitation systems, which has resulted in harmful contamination of water resources and increased floods.

Overall the agricultural drains receive the bulk of the treated and untreated domestic pollution load. As a result many canals now also are contaminated with wastewater pollutants. Apart from being the largest consumer of water, agriculture is also a major water polluter. This means a large number of organic and inorganic substances disturb the water quality, which are the main causes of eutrophication of the water body. They also proved to be powerful stimulants to algal growth and consequently formation of "algal blooms".

COMPOSITION OF TYPICAL WASTEWATER

It is a complex mixture of natural organic and inorganic materials as well as man-made compounds. Three quarters of organic carbon in sewage are present as carbohydrates, fats, proteins, amino acids, and volatile acids. The inorganic constituents include large concentrations of sodium, calcium, potassium, magne- sium, chlorine, sulphur, phosphate, bicarbonate, ammonium salts and heavy metals.

MICROBIOLOGICAL COMPOSITION OF SEWAGE

Wastewater environment is an ideal media for a wide range of microorganisms specially bacteria, viruses and protozoa. The majority is harmless and can be used in biological sewage treatment, but sewage also contains pathogenic microorganisms, which are excreted in large numbers by sick individuals and a symptomic carrier. Bacteria which cause cholera, typhoid and tuberculosis; viruses which cause infectious hepatitis; protozoa which cause dysentery and the eggs of parasitic worms are all found in sewage.

SEWAGE TREATMENT PROCESSES

In this review we will discuss about microalgae waste water treatment other than the conventional waste water treatment methods.

Microalgae for Wastewater Treatment

Bio-treatment with microalgae is particularly attractive because of their photosynthetic capabilities, converting solar energy into useful biomasses and incorporating nutrients such as nitrogen and phosphorus causing eutrophication.

The algal systems can treat human sewage, livestock wastes, agro-industrial wastes and industrial wastes. Also, microalgal systems for the treatment of other wastes such as piggery effluent, the efûuent from food processing factories and other agricultural wastes have been studied. Also, algae based system for the removal of toxic minerals such as lead, cadmium, mercury, scandium, tin, arsenic and bromine are also being developed. The technology and biotechnology of microalgal mass culture have been much discussed. Algal systems have traditionally been employed as a tertiary process. They have been proposed as a potential secondary treatment system.

Tertiary treatment process removes all organic ions. It can be accomplished biologically or chemically. The biological tertiary treatment appears to perform well compared to the chemical processes which are in general too costly to be implemented in most places and which may lead to secondary pollution. However, each additional treatment step in a wastewater system greatly increases the total cost. A complete tertiary process aimed at removing ammonia, nitrate and phosphate will thus be about four times more expensive than primary treatment.

Microalgal cultures offer an elegant solution to tertiary and quinary treatments due to the ability of microalgae to use inorganic nitrogen and phosphorus for their growth. And also, their capacity to remove heavy metals, as well as some toxic organic compounds, therefore, does not lead to secondary pollution. Amongst beneficial characteristics they produce oxygen, have a disinfecting effect due to increase in pH during photosynthesis. Algae can be used in wastewater treatment for a range of purposes, some of which are used for the removal of coliform bacteria, reduction of both chemical and biochemical oxygen demand, removal of N and/or P, and also for the removal of heavy metals.

Factors Affecting Algal Growth and Nutrient Removal

Algal growth and nutrient uptake are not only affected by the availability of nutrients, they also depend on complex interactions among physical factors such as pH, light intensity, temperature and biotic factors. The first biotic factor significantly influencing algal growth is the initial density, it is expected that the higher the algal density, the better the growth and the higher the nutrient removal efficiency. However, the high algal density would lead to self-shading, an accumulation of autoinhibitors, and a reduction in photosynthetic efficiency.

Algae as a Monitor of Water Quality

During the last three decades several investigations have described the algal bioassays in response to environmental perturbations and their use as indicative organisms of water quality. In 1959, Palmer published a composite rating of organisms such as *Euglena, Oscillatoria, Chlamydomonas, Scenedesmus, Chlorella, Nitzschia* and *Navicula,* which could be used as indicators of water pollution, whereas the presence of different organisms such as *Lemanea, Stigeoclonium* and certain species of *Micrasterias, Staurastrum, Pinnularia, Meridion* and *Surirella* would indicate that the water sample would be considered unpolluted.

CONCLUSION

- Algae can be used in wastewater treatment for a range of purposes, including:
  1. reduction of BOD.
  2. removal of N and/or P.
  3. inhibition of coliforms.
  4. removal of heavy metals
- The high concentration of N and P in most wastewaters also means these wastewaters may possibly be used as cheap nutrient sources for algal biomass production. This algal biomass could be used for:

1. methane production.
2. composting.
3. production of liquid fuels (pseudo-vegetable fuels).
4. as animal feed or in aquaculture.
5. production of fine chemicals.

REFERENCES

1. Abdel-Raouf, N., Ibraheem, I.B.M., Hammouda, O., 2003. Eutro-phication of River Nile as Indicator of Pollution. In: Al-Azhar Bull. of Sci., Proceeding of 5th Int. Sci. Conf. 25-27 March 2003, pp. 293-306.
2. Abel, P.D., 1989. Water Pollution Biology. Ellis Horwood Series in Wastewater Technology. Ellis Horwood Ltd., John Wiley & Sons, Chichester.
3. Baeza-Squiban, A., Bouaicha, N., Santa-Maria, A., Marano, F., 1990. Demonstration of the Excretion by Dunaliella Bioculata of Esterases Implicated in the Metabolism of Deltamethrin, a Pyrethroid Insecticide. Bull Environ. Contam. 45, 39-45.
4. Kiran, B., Kaushik, A., Kaushik, C.P., 2007. Biosorption of Cr (VI) by Native Isolate of Lyngbya Putealis (HH-15) in the Presence of Salts. J. Hazard. Mater. 141, 662-667.
5. Pearson, H.W., Mara, D.D., Bartone, C.R., 1987a. Guidelines for the Minimum Evaluation of the Performance of Full-scale Waste Stabilization Ponds. Water Res. 21 (9), 1067-1075.

Pages: 62-70

WASTE MANAGEMENT AND ENVIRONMENTAL HEALTH

Edited by: **Dr. B. Tabassum; Dr. Priya Bajaj & Dr. Pawan Kumar 'Bharti'**

ISBN: 978-93-5056-777-7

Edition: **2016**

Published by: **Discovery Publishing House Pvt. Ltd., New Delhi (India)**

Histopathological and Oxygen Consumption Alteration Induced by Toxicity of Dimethoate on Gills of Fish, *channa gachua*

Qaisur Rehman[1] and B. Tabassum[2]

ABSTRACT

Behavioral alterations like uncoordinated movements, erratic swimming, convulsions, excess mucus secretion, decreased opercular movements, loss of balance, drowning and change in body pigmentation became more apparent with increase in duration of exposure at all test concentration. The results of the water quality of the tap water used in the bioassay are in the normal range and suggest that parameters of the test water were not the cause of fish mortality. However, temperature, hardness, pH, alkalinity and biological factors such as sex, age, health, weight and physiological status are reported to have profound effects

[1]Department of Zoology, Vinoba Bhave University, Jharkhand - 825 301

[2]Department of Zoology, Govt Raza PG College, Rampur *Email:* qaisur.rahman@gmail.com

Corresponding Author: Qaisur Rahman, Department of Zoology, Vinoba Bhave University, Hazari Bagh, Jharkhand- 825301 *E-mail:* qaisur.rehman@gmail.com *Mob. No. :* +919430784729

on the acute toxicity of pesticides in *Channa gachua*. Toxicity of dimethoate is relatively lower when compared to other air breathing fishes. In the present investigation the histopathological effects of dimethoate in *Channa gachua* were exposed to sublethal concentration of i.e. 1/10th of 96 hour LC_{50} (0.599 ppm) for 30 days for study of histopathology and oxygen consumption. The histo pathological studies revealed pathological changes in the gills. The rate of oxygen consumption was also found to be increased initially up to 48 hours then decreased up to end of experiment. The details will be discussed in this paper.

Key words: Histopathology, Dimethoate, oxygen consumption, *Channa gachua*.

INTRODUCTION

While liberal use of chemical fertilizers and synthetic pesticides helped in ensuring food security to rising population, it inflicted severe injury to the environment especially to the health of soil and aquatic ecosystem. Non target organisms including fish suffer from pesticide pollution directly or and through food chain in water bodies receiving industrial effluents and runoff water from agricultural fields. Most pesticides used in agriculture and in hygiene programmes are non selective, more or less persistent and bio accumulate in the food chain and pose great danger to the health of non target organism in fresh water. Although mostly pesticides occur at low concentrations in ponds and other water bodies, they create serious problems for non-target aquatic biota, especially the fishes, due to their extensive range of biological activity, affinity and stability. Fishes are one of the most susceptible animals to pesticide pollution because of their anatomy and physiology.

Fishes live in intimate contact with surrounding water through their gills and branchial surface comprises over half the surface area of the body. Only a few microns thick delicate gill epithelium separates the internal environment of fish from external aquatic environment which makes the fish very susceptible to aquatic pollutants.

Therefore, contamination of water bodies by pesticides causes acute and chronic poisoning of fish and results in severe damage to vital organs (Singh *et. al.*, 2009). Dimethoate is a broad spectrum systemic organophosphate insecticide active against acaridae, aphididae, aleyrodidae, coccodidea, coleoptera, collembola, diptera, lepidoptera, pseudococcidae and thyanoptera in cotton, cereals, fruits, vegetables, tea, coffee, tobacco and pastures (Aysal *et. al.,* 2004). Like other organophosphates, dimethoate is an inhibitor of acetyl cholinesterase and causes accumulation of acetylcholine in nerve tissue and effecter organs with the principal site of action being the peripheral nervous system. The accumulation of acetylcholine results in a prolonged stimulation of the cholinergic receptors downstream leading to intense activation of autonomic nervous system, which depending upon the severity of acetyl cholinesterase inhibition results in tremors, convulsion, respiratory arrest and death .Though the organophosphate pesticide may disappear rapidly from the body either by hydrolysis or elimination, long term and repeated exposure to these pesticides have cumulative effect on fish.

In the aquatic environment the pesticides pollute the ecosystem and find their way into the body of an aquatic animals by means of gills, digestive tract and general body surface. Some pesticides accumulate in different tissues of body and produce toxic effects. In fishes it is observed that the organs are affected due to foreign bodies or toxic materials causing loss of equilibrium, irregular movements, and increase in opercular movements, imbalance and finally leading to death. Histopathology deals with the study of pathological changes induced in the microscopical structure of body tissue. Any peculiar alteration of cells may indicate the presence of disease or the effect of toxic substance. In fishes, it is observed that the external organ get affected due to toxic chemical causing irregular movement, loss of equilibrium, increased opercular movement, shedding of scales, lesion on head and gills, finally leading to death.

MATERIALS AND METHODS

Channa gachua is also known as an air breathing murrel fish belonging to the family Channidae of the order Channiformes. It is found in estuaries and freshwaters of India. It has a very good flavour and is popular as food. This fish has dual mode gas exchange mechanism as it extracts oxygen from water through gills and from air by accessory respiratory organs. The accessory respiratory organs comprise one pair of suprabranchial chambers.

Live specimens of *Channa gachua* were procured from local fish dealers at Hazaribag (Latitude 25° 59′N and Longitude 85° 22′E) and maintained in large glass aquaria size (90 x 60 x 60cm) with continuous flow of water. The specimens were fed on chopped goat liver daily during a minimum acclimation period of 15 days in the laboratory. Routine oxygen consumption from air and still water was measured in a closed glass respirometer containing 3 litres of water (initial O_2 content = 6.5 mg O_2/litre; pH = 7.2) and 0.51 ML of air (Fig. 6.1).

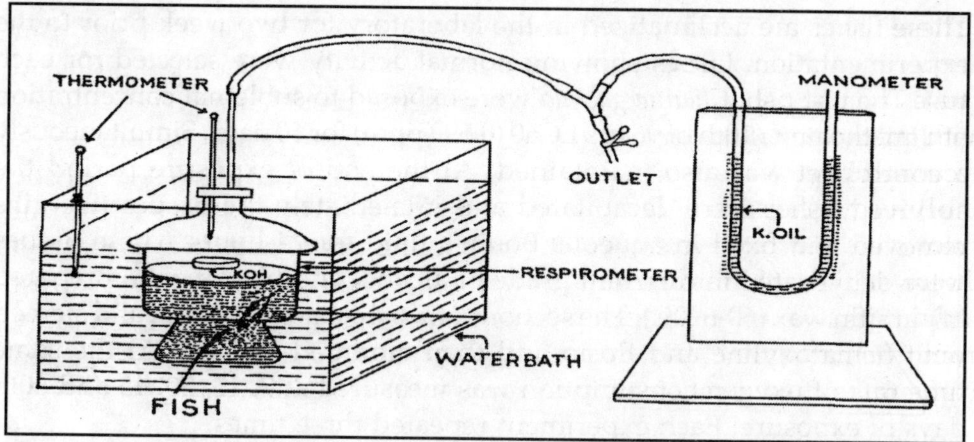

Fig. 6.1: **Experimental Set up for the Measurements of Dual mode of Oxygen uptake in *Channa gachua***

The fish had free access to air through a small semi circular hole (10 cm diameter) in a disc float. Carbosorb (B.D.H) or KOH in a petridish placed on the float absorbed CO_2. Thus the fish could exchange gases with water by way of its gills as well as with the air using the suprabranchial chamber. The air phase of respirometer was connected to a differential manometer. Movement of the manometer fluid follow uptake of oxygen when the CO_2 is absorbed by "Carbosorb" (KOH). The fish were acclimatized to the respirometers for at least 12 hours before the readings were taken. The concentration of dissolved oxygen in the water was estimated by Winkler's volumetric method (Welch, 1948).The oxygen uptake through gills was calculated from the difference between the oxygen levels of the ambient water in the respirometer before and after the experiment and the reading of volume of water in the respirometer. The oxygen uptake from air was measured and calculated from the reading of volume change in the manometer and by the use of the combined gas law equations and vapour pressure. Mean values of oxygen consumption in a series of observations, on each fish at standard temperature pressure dry and standard errors were calculated.

The experiments were conducted at 29.0 ± 1.5°C. The pH of the ambient water was measured by an electronic pH meter (Systronics). The respiratory chambers were thermostated by immersion in a temperature controlled water bath. However, sexually mature fishes of almost same weight group (40-50g) were used Qaisur Rahman (2011) respectively.

For the study of histopathology and oxygen consumption the live test fish were cleaned by using 0.1% KmnO4 to avoid the dermal infection.

These fishes are acclimatized in the laboratory for two week prior to the experimentation. Fishes showing normal activity were selected for each test. The test fish, *Channa gachua* were exposed to sublethal concentration of dimethoate 1/10th of 96 hrs LC50 (0.599 ppm) for 60 days. Simultaneously a control set was also maintained. At the end of exposure period the survived fishes were decapitated and immediately the tissues like gills removed and fixed in aqueous Bouin's fluid for 24 hours. These tissues were dehydrated in different grade of alcohol and blocks were prepared in paraffin wax (60-620C). The sections of 5-6 thickness were cut and stained with hematoxyline and Eosin and then mounted in DPX. At the same time rate of oxygen consumption was measured at 7, 15, 30, 45 and 60th days of exposure. Each experiment repeated three times.

RESULTS AND DISCUSSION

In the present investigation, the histopathological and oxygen consumption alterations induced by treatment of dimethoate in tissues like gills. The gills of the fish exposed to dimethoate exhibited marked histopathological changes. The main features observed in gills exposed to sublethal concentration of dimethoate were partial degeneration of epithelium of secondary gill lamellae. In some place adjacent secondary gill lamellae appeared to adhere each other. Fusion of secondary gill lamellae resulting in reduction of respiratory surface and vacuolization was also recorded. No change was observed in primary gill lamellae. The effect of dimethoate on gill to different exposure period is shown in plate.

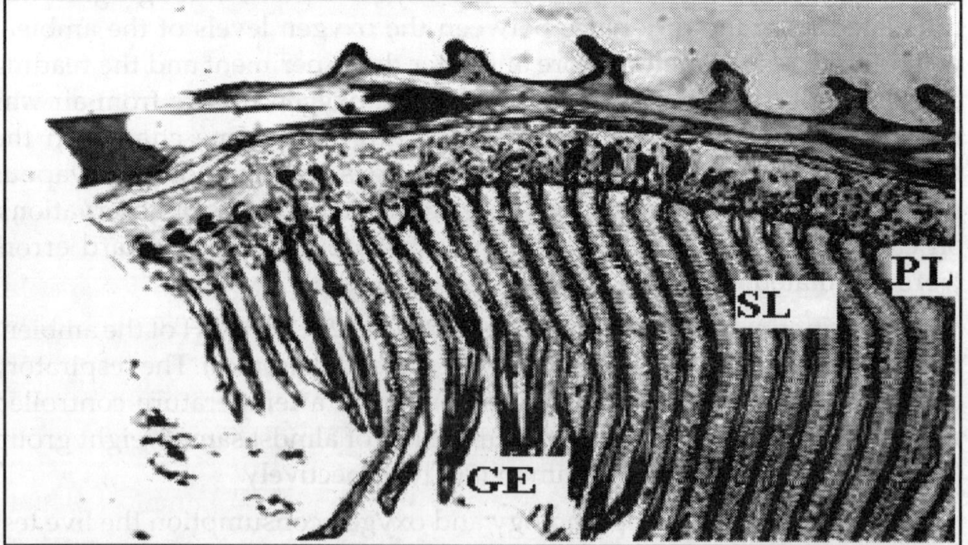

Fig. 6.2: **Showing the Gills Structure with Dimethoate in *Channa gachua***

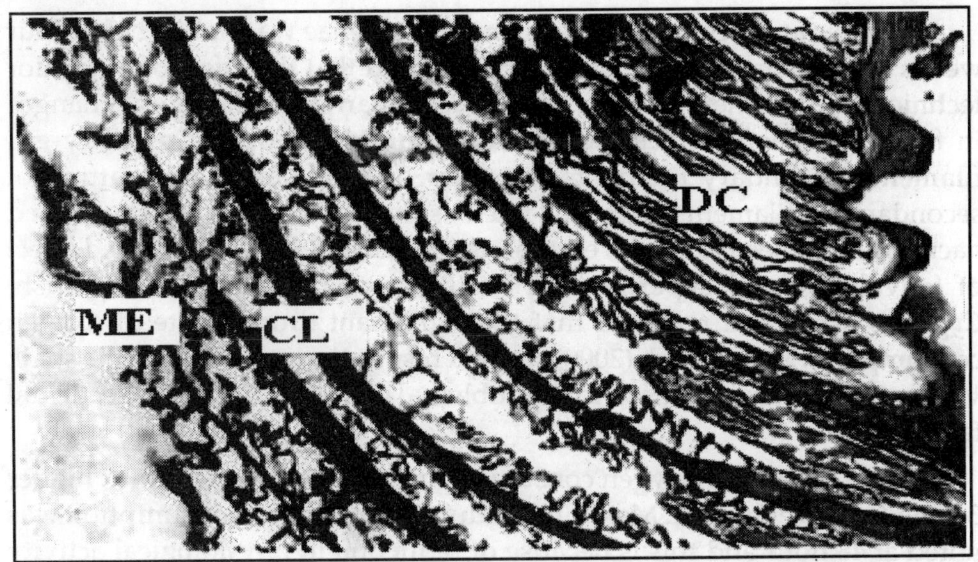

Fig. 6.3: **Experimental Fish Gill, HE, X 50, CL-Curled Lamellae, DC-Damaged Cells ME-Marked Edema in *Channa gachua*.**

The effect of dimethoate on the rate of oxygen consumption in 1, 7, 15, 30, 45 and 60 days exposure period is 0.6242, 0.5815, 0.6566, 0.5812, 0.6347 and 0.6514 in 0.0 ppm but in 0.599 ppm it was 0.5214, 0.7783, 0.8148, 0.6540, 0.5165 and 0.3847 mg/lit/g weight of fish/hour respectively. The effect of dimethoate on the rate of oxygen consumption at 60 day exposure period and graphically represented in figure.The similar results was reported by various workers Rao *et. al.*, (1983), Pawar and katdare (1983) Ali (1982) Sunita Singh, *et. al.*,(1984), Oikari *et. al*. (1985) Choudhan and Pandy (1987) while studied on toxicity of various pesticides on freshwater fish. Srivastava and Srivastva (1984) studied effect of sublethal concentration of malthion chloride on the histopathology of the gills of *Channa gachua* and observed hyperplasia, hypertrophy vacillation in. Anithakumar and Sreeram Kumar (1995;1997) reported several histo pathological changes in kidney, liver, gills, intestine and ovary due to impact of industrial effluents in the fish, *Channa punctatus* and *Hetropneustes fossils*. Khan *et. al*. (2000) studied effect of heavy metal on histopathological structure of gill of crustaceans and stated that decline in the rate of oxygen consumption may be the result of formation of coagulated mucous over the gills and body surface of the crab. Rana and Eragi (2004) worked on histopathological alternation induced by pesticides on gill of mudskipper and reported that the exposure of fish for two weeks to cypermethrin resulted in the bulging and fusion of secondary lamellae, lifting of epithelial cells.

Necrosis and destruction of secondary lamellae was noticed after four weeks of exposure. Tilak *et. al.,* (2005) reported that the effect of butachlor technical and machete 50% EC has induced marked pathological changes in fish gills. The changes included the bulging of tips of primary gill filaments, secondary filaments lost their original shape and cutting of secondary gill filaments, pillar cell nucleus showed necrosis and developed vacuoles in the secondary gill epithelium. Malla Reddy (1987) studied effect of fenvalerate and cypermethrin on the oxygen consumption of fish, *Cyprinus carpio* and reported that the significant drop in rate of oxygen consumption. Thosar *et.al.,*(2000) studied respirations response of the snail, *Vivipara bengalensis*, exposed to the sublethal concentrations of insecticidal fenvalerate.

Fall in the rate of oxygen consumption in this case was more at higher 3.7 mg/L concentration. Maximum reduction in oxygen consumption was noted at 48 hour and this is because of reduction in physiological activity and damage caused to the gills. Sexena and Chauhan (2003) reported that the decrease in dissolved oxygen caused a stress and resulted in an increase in the rate of oxygen consumption by the fish while working on oxygen consumption in fish *Labeo rohita* (Ham) caused by distillery effluent. They stated that the inorganic and organic salts might have interfered with respiration in *Labeo rohita* by coagulation of gill mucous and caused asphyxiation as well as inhibition of enzyme system at mitochondrial level. This resulted in decreased in oxygen consumption. Waykar Bhalchandra and Lomte (2003) studied respiratory response of freshwater bivalve, *Parreysia cylindrica* to endosulfan and reported that the rate of oxygen consumption was found to be decreased with increase in exposure period the decrease was maximum in chronic exposure as compared to acute expsoure. Prashant *et. al.,* (2003) studied effect of cypermethrin on toxicity and oxygen consumption in the freshwater fish *Cirrhinus mrigala,* and reported that the decreased in level of oxygen consumption exposed to lethal concentration for 1, 2, 3 and 4 days and also in sublethal concentration of 1, 7, 14 and 21 days. It is may be due to the respiratory dystress as a consequence of the impairment of oxidative metabolism.

Arun Kumar (2007) worked on effects of different ratio of oxygen and water on the survival of gold fish *Carassius auratus* and reported that dissolved oxygen 7.2mg/h recorded in all the treatments during the start of the experimental period and latter these parameters gradually decreased at the end of the experimental period. On above literature on the rate of oxygen consumption and histopathology shows that rate of oxygen consumption decreased as concentration of toxicant and time of exposure period increased. It may be due to reduction in respiratory potential of gill tissues probably caused by tissues damage under pesticide tress or it may be due to suppression of metabolic activity of fish.At lethal concentrations, dimethoate toxicity like other organophosphate is rapidly reflected in behavioral alterations of exposed fishes. Decrease in opercular rate appears to be an effort of exposed fish to reduce contact of gill epithelium with the poison. To compensate for the loss of oxygen uptake from water fish frequently swims to the surface to gulp air. Increased mucous secretion probably helps in countering irritating effect of dimethoate in skin and mucous membrane. Excitement, hyperactivity and abnormal jerky swimming observed in exposed fishes may be caused by accumulation of neurotransmitter in neuromuscular junctions. Loss of balance and drowning reflect the progression towards death as fish succumbs to the continued high exposure of dimethoate. Similar alterations in behavior of dimethoate exposed fish have been reported earlier in *Heteropneustes fossilis* (Pandey *et. al.*, 2009) and *Cyprinus carpio* Singh *et. al.*, (2009) Qaisur and Choudhary (2013) respectively. It is concluded that dimethoate is highly toxic to fish which is swiftly reflected in behavioral alterations culminating in death. Further studies on toxicity of dimethoate and its combinations with other pesticides in laboratory and field may help in deciding judicious use of pesticides.

REFERENCES

1. Ali, S.M., Ilyas R and Mokashi, N.V. (1985): Oxygen Consumption of Fish *Channa gachua* (Hamilton) After Exposure to Dimacron and Aldicrab. Geobios 2: 44-48.
2. Anitha Kumari and Shree Ram Kumar (1997): Effect of Polluted Water on Histochemical Localization of Carbohydrate in a Freshwater Teleost, *Channa punctatus* (Bloch) from Hussian.
3. Anitha Kumari, S. and Sreeram Kumar, N., (1995): Histopathological Lesions Caused by Industrial Effluents in Kidney, Liver and Gill of Fish, *Hetropneustes fossilis* in Hussain Sagar, Lake Hydrabad, India. Bull. Pure. App. Sci. 14(2): 57-64.
4. Arun Kumar, J. (2007): Effects of Different Ratio of Oxygen and Water on the Survival of Gold Fish (*Carassius auratus)* J. Ecotoxicol. Environ. Monit. 17(2): 197-199.
5. Aruna Devi P.S. and K. Nagrajan (2006): Impact of Distillery Effluent on Certain Physiological Aspects of the Indian Major Fresh Water Carp, *Labeo rohita,* Geobios. (12): 111-115
6. Aysal P., Tiryaki, O. and Tuncbilek, A.S., (2004): Dimethoate Residues in Tomato and Tomato Products. Bull. Environ. Contam.Toxicol.73: 351-357.
7. Choudhan M.S. and Pandey, A.K. (1987): Histopathological Changes in the Gills of *Punctius ticto* J. Environ. Biol. 24: 67-71.

8. Pandey R.K., Singh R.N., Singh, S. Singh, N.N. and Das, V.K., (2009): Acute Toxicity Bioassay of Dimethoate on Freshwater Air Breathing Catfish *Heteropneustes fossilis* (Bloch). J. Environ. Biol. 30: 437-440.

9. Qaisur Rahman (2011): Studies on Some Factors Affecting Aerial and Aquatic Respiration in an Air Breathing Fish *Channa gachua* (Ham.) Ph.D. Thesis, Vinoba Bhave University, Hazaribag, Jharkhand, India.

10. Qaisur Rahman and Choudhary, Shamim Akhter (2013): Effect of Zinc Cyanide on the Behaviour and Oxygen Consumption in Air Breathing Fish *Channa gachua*. J.Res.Dev.13: 67-79.

11. Sagar lake, Hydrabad, Andhra Pradesh, Poll. Res. 16(3): 197-200.

12. Singh R.N., Pandey R.K., Singh N.N. and Das V.K., (2009): Acute Toxicity and Behavioral Responses of Common Carp Cyprinus Carpio (Linn.) to an Organophosphate (Dimethoate). World. J. Zool. 4: 70-75.

13. Welch, P.S. (1948): Limnological Methods Mc Graw Hill Book Co. Inc New York, London. pp. 206-213.

***Pages:* 71-78**

WASTE MANAGEMENT AND ENVIRONMENTAL HEALTH

***Edited by:* Dr. B. Tabassum; Dr. Priya Bajaj & Dr. Pawan Kumar 'Bharti'**

ISBN: 978-93-5056-777-7

***Edition:* 2016**

***Published by:* Discovery Publishing House Pvt. Ltd., New Delhi (India)**

Managing Biodiversity, Waste and Air Quality

Altamash Khan

INTRODUCTION

Sustainable development through finding a balance between environmental, social and economic needs is the demand for today. If we are serious about minimizing our environmental impact, we need to manage our 'whole of farm' operations. The urban area expanded by 171% worldwide between 1950 and 2000, and some studies suggest that it may increase by another 150% to 2030. Nearly half the world's population now lives in urban areas, and this proportion is expected to grow to 60% by 2030. About 89% of the total projected urban population growth of 1.8 billion people from 2005 to 2030 will occur in non-OECD countries. Continuing urban sprawl will put pressure on the environment through

Department of Zoology, Govt. P.G. College, Bilaspur, Rampur
Email: altamash.gulzar@gmail.com
Corresponding Author: Altamash Khan, C/o Aslam Khan, Pakka Bagh, Mazar Shah Dargahi Sahab, Rampur (UP) - 244 901, *Email:* altamash.gulzar@gmail.com, *Mob.:* +91-9760654243

land use stress, fragmentation of natural habitats, long-term soil degradation, and increases in greenhouse gas and air pollution emissions.

Biodiversity has high economic value. Some of the more obvious sources of value include: bio-prospecting, carbon sequestration, watersheds and tourism. These are direct sources of biodiversity value and do not include indirect aspects such as protection against major pathogens, sources of innovation in agricultural production, the existence value of biodiversity, etc. The pharmacological value of biodiversity may be in the multi-billion dollar range; a successful product can be worth USD 5 to USD 10 billion per year in revenues net of production costs, with a present value over its life of perhaps USD 50 to USD 100 billion. Indeed, finding just a small number of additional blockbuster drugs from the remaining biodiversity would justify significant conservation for bio-prospecting. Biodiversity's carbon storage value may also be in the tens of billions of dollars since it is a significant reservoir of carbon: there are now markets for carbon that allow the implicit pricing of stored carbon. The services provided by biodiversity through watersheds and charismatic megafauna are harder to estimate in total, but again clearly run to billions of dollars. New York City alone saved hundreds of millions of dollars by maintaining its source watershed rather than building a water purification plant. The costs of biodiversity loss through continued policy inaction will thus be significant in both measurable economic loss and difficult-to-measure non-marketed terms. Getting a precise total figure for that loss is not possible, but there is good reason to suspect that it is large. (Heal, 2000)

Good practice extends beyond the key production practices. From the outset, following four management modules has been combined (EnviroVeg Manual, second edition):

- Biodiversity Management
- Waste Management
- Water Quality Management

Waste Management

Vegetable production generates waste. Waste should be managed to conform to relevant regulations and minimize environmental harm. Waste management on the farm should incorporate strategies to reduce, re-use and recycle so that disposal of waste is kept to a minimum. This review outlines a range of responsible waste management strategies that include:

- Waste storage
- Minimizing waste
- Responsible disposal

There are also guidelines on preparing an action plan using the 'Plan-Do-Check-Review' cycle of continuous improvement (Freshcare Ltd., 2007)

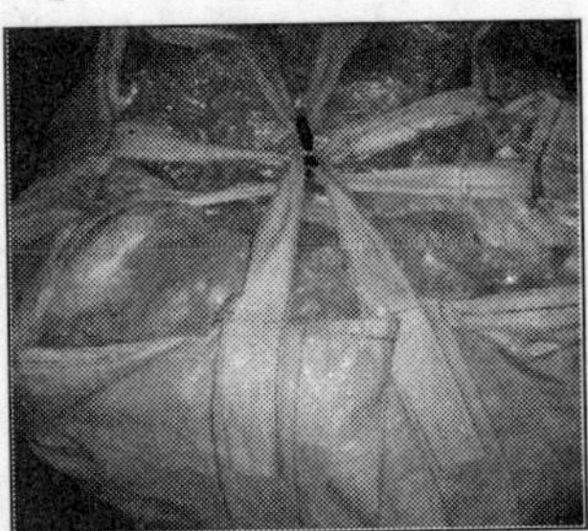

Air Quality Management

Odour, dust, smoke and noise, generated on your property, can affect your neighbors. Responsible air quality management should include strategies to minimize odour, dust, smoke and noise as well as minimize the production of greenhouse gas (EnviroVeg, 2007).

- **Odour:** Common sources of odour are animal manure, mulch, chemicals and waste. Odours affecting neighbours can be reduced by storing sources away from boundaries, managing manures and crop waste, choosing low odour products and managing waste appropriately.

- **Dust:** Reduce dust by minimizing bare-soil areas, establishing windbreaks, avoiding cultivation of dry soil and irrigating bare-soil areas during dry, windy conditions.
- **Smoke:** Avoid burning waste. If you must burn, ensure that you conform to local regulations and plan to burn when the wind direction will ensure minimal impact on your neighbours.
- **Noise:** Manage your farm activities to minimize the risk of noise. Maintain machinery and equipment, including efficiency of noise abatement components (mufflers etc.)

Natural Diversity Threats

Biodiversity in the earth continues to face pressures from a large and increasing population. The demand for housing, coupled with inappropriate urban design, is resulting in the extinction of many species

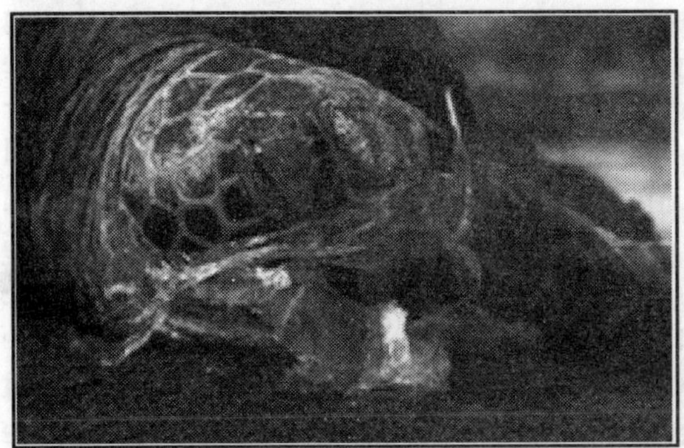

of plants and animals, through fragmentation and land clearing. Climate change is having a direct and indirect impact on biodiversity. Changes to climate can directly affect species and the ecosystems in which they live, through changes to ambient temperature, rainfall, winds and extreme events. Indirect effects can be caused by changes to fire frequency and timing, the spread and intensity of diseases such as dieback (*Phytophthora cinnamomi*), competition and predation, and altering water flows. Lower rainfall and increased pumping from the Gnangara mound have reduced the water table, which is a possible cause of some recent vegetation death. Many species, along with their habitats and ecological communities are threatened, including wetlands of international importance and migratory bird habitats. Species management now focuses on a 'whole of landscape' approach, rather than concentrating on individual species in isolation. Preserving an adequate and representative set of reserves will enrich the region by maintaining the full range of endemic landform, soil and vegetation complexes. Ecosystem integrity is essential to the survival of species and requires the creation of reasonably large inter-linked areas – not just the protection of small, isolated remnants.

Ecosystem services can be defined as the benefits people obtain from ecosystems. Ecosystems on agricultural land have been deliberately modified to enhance their capacity to provide products desired by society. Vegetable growers can implement a number of strategies to manage on-farm biodiversity. The first step is to understand that biodiversity helps to support a healthy environment in a number of ways: Vegetation helps to clean air and water and moderate our climate Soil organisms or the Soil Food Web (Soil and Water Conservation Society, 2000) return minerals to the soil and maintain soil quality and performance. Many plants depend on insects for pollination Birds and insects can help control pests. Vegetation and waterways provide habitat for wildlife, insects and other organisms Vegetation provides shade, shelter and privacy Native vegetation contributes to the character of the Australian landscape Air quality management Odour, dust, smoke and noise, generated on your property, can affect your neighbors. Responsible air quality management should include strategies to minimize odour, dust, smoke and noise as well as minimize the production of greenhouse gas (EnviroVeg, 2007).

Dumping

Dumping in this assessment is defined as "The deliberate disposal in the maritime area of wastes or other matter from vessels or aircraft, from offshore installations, and any deliberate disposal in the maritime area of vessels or aircraft, offshore installations and offshore pipelines". The term does not include disposal in accordance with MARPOL 73/78 or other applicable international law of wastes or other matter incidental to, or derived from, the normal operations of vessels or aircraft or offshore installations (other than wastes or other matter transported by or to vessels of offshore installations for the purpose of disposal of such wastes or other matter or derived from the treatment of such wastes or other matter on such vessels or aircraft of offshore installations). The different categories of wastes or other matter considered in this assessment are:

(a) Dredged material;

(b) Inert materials of natural origin, that is solid, chemically unprocessed geological material the chemical constituents of which are unlikely to be released into the marine environment;

(c) Sewage sludge;

(d) Fish waste from industrial fish processing operations;

(e) Vessels or aircrafts.

Dumping activities may cause physical disturbance and may result in the redistribution, and possibility of changing the form, of contamination. Physical disturbance includes increases in suspended matter, which affects primary production and growth of filter-feeding organisms, burial of benthic organisms and changes in substrate character, which may affect benthic communities. Several effects of the disposal of dredged sediment at sea are distinguished in the literature review. The main effects are related to:

- chemical disturbances;
- increased nutrient input;
- change in sediment structure;
- enhanced sedimentation (burial and smothering);
- increased turbidity;
- enhanced suspended particulate matter.

Dumpsites tend to be in estuarine, coastal or near-shore areas in the vicinity of dredging locations (harbors and shipping channels). Two hundred and thirty seven dumpsites were licensed throughout the Convention Area in the mid 1990s. This increased to 383 in 2005. This increase is partly an artifact of incomplete reporting in the mid 1990s, but there has also been an increase in capital and maintenance dredging for major port extension projects. In future there might be a further increase in dredging due to increasing ship traffic and the use of bigger ships which require deeper and wider navigation routes, as well as an increased maintenance dredging requirement for enlarged port facilities. However, available data do not show any specific trends in the OSPAR Maritime Area.

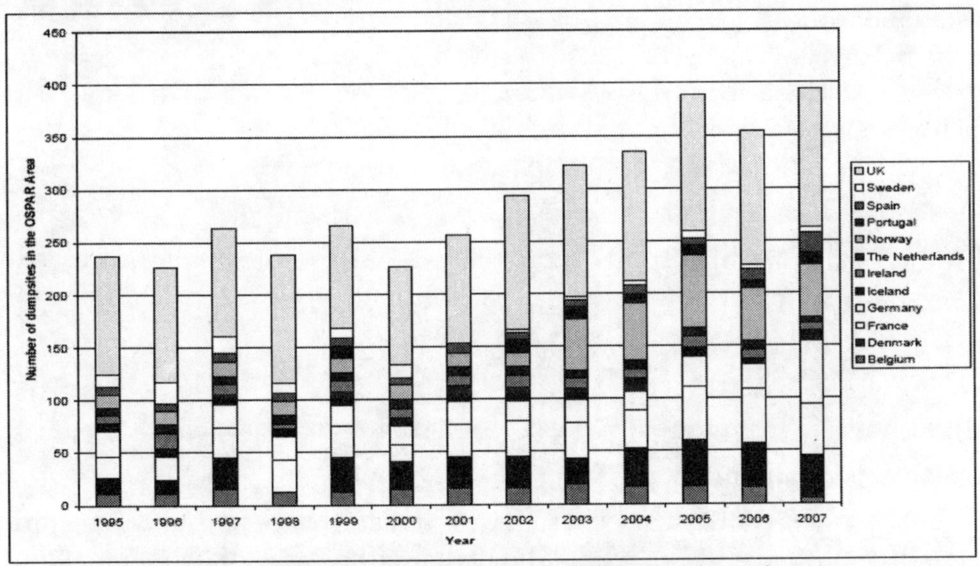

Overview of the Number and Distribution of Dumpsites within the OSPAR Area

Source: **Annual OSPAR Reports on Dumping of Wastes at Sea**

REFERENCES

1. Australian Museum Online, Australia's Biodiversity, 2005.
2. Department of Agriculture and Food Western Australia (DAFWA). Farming for the Future Management Baseline Horticulture Industry, Working document, July 2007.
3. EnviroVeg Manual, Edition 2. A USVEG Ltd, 2007.
4. Freshcare Ltd. Environmental Training Workbook, Version 3, August 2007.
5. Hussey, B.M. and Wallace, K.J. Managing your Bush Land. Department of Conservation and Land Management, Western Australia, 1993.
6. Perth Region NRM, Natural Diversity Programme, 2007.
7. Polybrominated Diphenylethers (PBDEs) Significant New Use Rules (SNUR), March 20, 2012, Implementation of EPA's 2010 Action Plan on PBDEs
8. Shearer, B.L., Crane, C.E. and Cochrane, A. Quantification of the Susceptibility of the Native Flora of the South-West Botanical Province, Western Australia, to *Phytophthora cinnamomi*. Australian Journal of Botany; 52: 435-443, 2004.
9. Soil and Water Conservation Society. Soil Biology Primer, 2000.
10. South Africa Regulation Gazette No. 10232, Regulasiekoerant, Vol. 589; Pretoria, 10 July 2014.
11. Tugel, A.J., A.M. Lewandowski, and D. Happe-vonArb, eds. 2000. Soil Biology Primer. Ankeny, IA: Soil and Water Conservation Society.
12. http://www.amonline.net.au/biodiversity
13. http//www.swancatchmentcouncil.org

Pages: 79-99

WASTE MANAGEMENT AND ENVIRONMENTAL HEALTH

Edited by: **Dr. B. Tabassum; Dr. Priya Bajaj & Dr. Pawan Kumar 'Bharti'**

ISBN: 978-93-5056-777-7

Edition: **2016**

Published by: **Discovery Publishing House Pvt. Ltd., New Delhi (India)**

Problems of Garbage Management in Urban Environment *A Micro Level Study in Rampur, Uttar Pradesh*

Faiza Naeem

INTRODUCTION

One of the major pollutants of our environment is the solid waste that is routinely generated in our townships, cities and metropolitan areas etc. The major proportions of solid waste consist of garbage produced by households and commercial establishments like shops, markets and mandies etc. Garbage is composed of everyday items that are discarded by the public. The management and disposal of solid waste is traditionally the major responsibility of local bodies like town areas, municipal boards and municipal corporations etc. With the growing population, urbanization, and industrialization the problem of solid waste management is becoming

Department of Zoology, Govt. Raza PG College, Rampur - 244901 (UP) (India)
Email: faizanaeem.vict@gmail.com

Corresponding Author: Faiza Naeem, C/o Sayed Saeed Ahmad, Near Ek Minara Masjid, Talab Mulla Iram, Rampur - 244901 (UP) (India) *Mob.:* +918791009974
Email: faizanaeem.vict@gmail.com

the matter of concern for the environmentalists all over the world. The present study deals with the problem of disposal and management of garbage in Rampur city.

RAMPUR CITY

Rampur city is situated about 182 Km from Delhi (National capital) in the east and 314 km from Lucknow in the west. It is connected by national Highway 24 which runs from west to east. Rampur city is the headquarters of district Rampur, which is part of administrative division of Moradabad in Uttar Pradesh.

The city of Rampur has its own municipal board. The municipal board covers an area of 20.0 sqkm and a population of 3.5 lakhs which includes a floating population of about 30,000. The city has been divided into 43 wards. Each ward is represented by an elected member. Thus there are 43 elected members and 5 nominated members. The board is headed by a chairman who is directly elected by the electorates of Rampur city. The primary responsibility of municipal board is sanitation, lightening and water supply in the city.

METHOD

The study is a kind of survey largely based on field observation and data collected from the local municipal board. Our study is of micro level in nature which aims at bringing into focus and highlighting very minute details of garbage management in average city like Rampur in Uttar Pradesh. In order to comprehend and understand the very basic and primary issues of the related problem, a micro level study is definitely a better instrument of investigation of the problem like the one that is under our study.

In order to keep the city clean, the disposal and management of garbage is of crucial importance. The collection and disposal of garbage is primarily the responsibility of municipal bodies of the concerned area. To maintain cleanliness and sanitation of the city, a regular staff at different levels of authorities and workers is maintained by the municipal board. The sanitary staff of Rampur municipal board comprises 15 sanitary karamcharies or garbage collectors in each ward. 1 supervisor called safai nayak in each ward. There are 7 safai inspectors, 2 chief sanitary inspectors. They are supervised and controlled by health officer and executive officer of municipal board. The overall administration and supervision of municipal board is the responsibility of the chairman. The ward members have an overriding supervisory status in their respective wards.

Fig. 8.1: Rampur Municipal Board

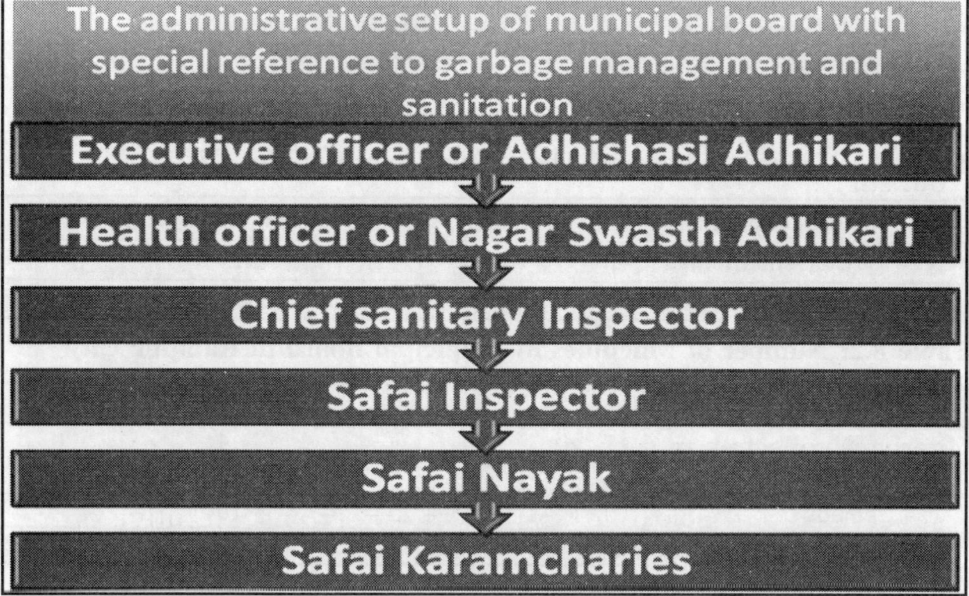

Fig. 8.2: Sequence of Sanitary Staff in Rampur Municipal Board

Although the sanitary workers or safai karamcharies, as they are called, are at the lowest rung of the workers hierarchy, they play very important role in garbage collection and its disposal. Every morning these workers go into the field and collect house garbage from door to door and carry the same in their hand carts to the nearby dumping points. Some of them sweep the streets and clean the drains and nullahs etc. They are supervised and directed by safai nayak. From dumping grounds the garbage is loaded with the help of JCB machines into trucks and trolleys specially meant for the purpose. The garbage is carried from dumping points to the trenching grounds which are located outside the city.

Fig. 8.3: Safai Karamchari at Work

Table 8.1: Disposal Sites and Their Number in Rampur City

Disposal Sites	Their Number
Collection Points	51
Trenching Grounds	2

Table 8.2: Number of Machines in Municipal Board in Rampur City

Machines	Number
JCB	4
Tractor trolley	10
Tempos	10
Road sweeping machine	1
Sewer cleaning machine	1
Jetting Machine	1

A

B

C

Fig. 8.4 (a, b & c): **Waste Collecting Machines of Rampur Municipal Board**

GARBAGE IN RAMPUR CITY

In Rampur average amount of Garbage generated every day is estimated to be 110-130 Metric tons. Major contents of garbage are as following:

- Used polythene bags
- Disposable items like cups, glasses, plates.
- Wrappers
- Plastic bottles
- Plastic containers
- Food leftovers
- Kitchen waste
- Rotten vegetables and fruits
- Green and dried twigs and leaves of plants
- Pieces of bidi patta
- Bones
- Animal excreta
- Stubs of cigarette and bidis
- Wrappers of gutka and pan masala
- Empty sachets of shampoo and detergent
- Pieces of glass, metals etc.

Table 8.3: Biodegradable and Non-biodegradable Contents of Garbage

Biodegradable Contents	Non-bioderadable Contents
Kitchen waste	Polythene bags
Green and dried twigs and leaves of plants	Empty sachets of shampoos and detergents
Animal excreta	Pieces of glass, metals etc.
Bones	Wrappers of gutka and pan masala
Stubs of bidis and cigarette	Plastic bottles
Sugarcane baggase	Plastic containers
Pices of bidi patta	Rubber, metal, and glass etc.
Food leftovers	Variety of plastic items
Rotten fruits and vegetables etc	Pieces of cloths

Garbage contents differ from area to area and from season to season as well as on special occasions like festivals. In posh areas like civil lines the contents of the garbage include mostly plastic items, wrappers of packed food items, cold drink containers, food leftovers, used tissues and waste paper etc. In old city areas the garbage contains used pieces of clothes, animal feces, polythene bags, bidi patta, stubs of bidi and cigarette rotten fruits and vegetables etc. During summer peels of mango, watermelon, and other fruits and vegetables inviting swarms of different kinds of flies is a regular seen on the dumping grounds. Similarly during winter piles of groundnut shells, sugarcane pieces and its baggase, half burnt cycle tyres and ashes are present in garbage.

Fig. 8.5: **(*a & b*): Garbage in Posh Areas of Rampur**

On occasions like Eid the waste from slaughtered animals is all thrown in the garbage in open without any proper treatment. This causes a lot of damage to the environment due to foul odour, diseases etc and inconvenience to the public. Likewise on occasions like Diwali crackers and other fire-works produce large amount of waste and also pollutes the environment. The packets of fireworks and the remains of used fire-works are found in the garbage.

SOURCES OF GARBAGE

Sources of garbage mainly include households, fruit and vegetable mandies, shops, market places etc. Households are the major source of garbage. Fruit and vegetable mandies also produce garbage. Garbage produced by fruits and vegetable mandies is mainly biodegradable consisting rotten fruits and vegetables and its packaging. Shops and markets are also the sources of garbage specially the eateries like tea shops, chat thellas etc.

Fig. 8.6: Garbage in Old City Areas of Rampur

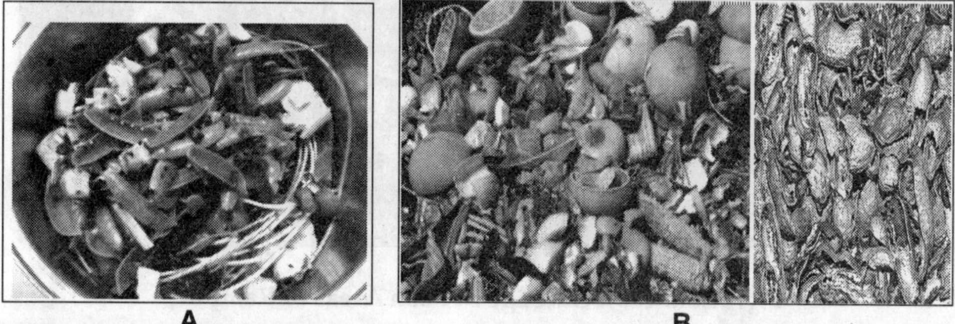

Fig. 8.7: (*a*) Garbage during Summer (*b*) Garbage during Winters

Fig. 8.8: Garbage on Occassions Like Eid

Fig. 8.9: **Garbage during Diwali**

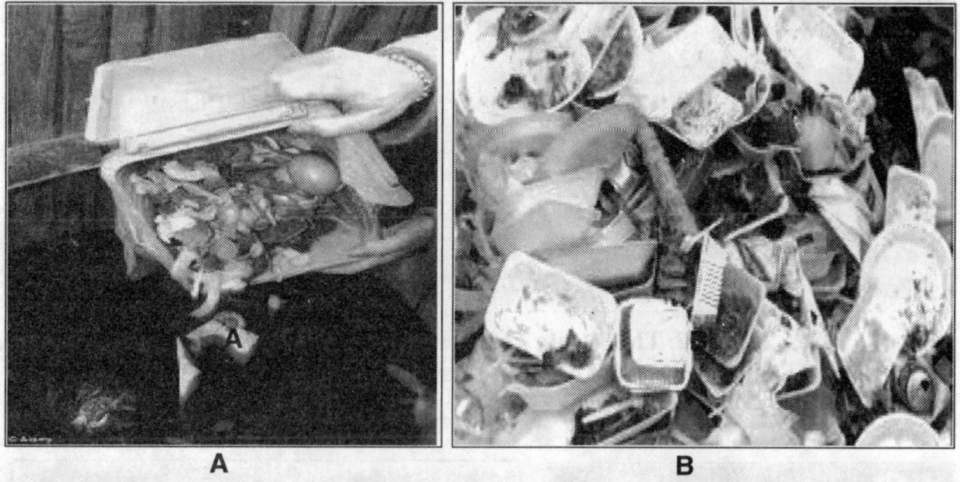

Fig. 8.10: **(*a*) Household Garbage** **(*b*) Garbage from Eateries**

DISPOSAL OF GARBAGE IN RAMPUR CITY

Garbage is collected from door to door by safai karamcharies. Some people specially the shop keepers throw the waste directly along the road side or into the adjoining drains and nullahs. Garbage collected from the primary sources is carried to the dumping points. From dumping points the waste is loaded into trucks and trolleys with the help of JCB machines and carried to major dumping grounds called trenches on the outskirts of the city.

Fig. 8.11: Safai Karamcharies Collecting Garbage from Door to Door

Fig. 8.12: The Waste Thrown Directly Along the Road Side or into the Adjoining Drains and Nullahs by People

Fig. 8.13: The Waste being Carried to Dumping Ground

Fig. 8.14: **The Waste being Loaded into Trucks and Trolleys with the help of JCB Machines**

An Overview of Sanitary Conditions in the City of Rampur

Inspite of the deployment of a large number of sanitary staff and the mechanical equipment available with the municipal board, the overall sanitary conditions in the city leaves much to be desired. Sanitary conditions differ from area to area, For example, In civil lines, the conditions are definitely much better than those found in old city areas specially on the periphery of the old city moreover the newly included areas in the municipal limit which were earlier rural are still in a bad shape.

PROBLEMS OF GARBAGE DISPOSAL AND ITS IMPACT ON ENVIRONMENT

Some of the major problems of garbage disposal in Rampur city and its impact on environment are listed below:

1. Though the dustbins have been placed at different points throughout the city by the municipal board but people are too lazy to dump their garbage into these dustbins usually the waste is seen around these dustbins. People are not careful in using these dustbins. In some areas since single dustbin is provided. When these dustbins become overloaded the waste start spilling out from it on the road.

Fig. 8.15: **Waste Spilling out on Road from Overloaded Dustbins**

Fig. 8.16: **Chocked Drainages**

Fig. 8.17: **Picture Showing Insensitivity of People that they Feel no Hesitation on Sitting Near the Places with Heaps of Garbage and Chocked Nullahs**

Fig. 8.18: **Garbage Providing Breeding and Feeding Ground for Mosquitoes, Flies and Rodents**

Most of the garbage is dumped along the road side, drains and nullahs. The non-cleaning of these drainages results in choking. People are so insensitive here that they feel no hesitation on sitting near the places with heaps of garbage and chocked nullahs as if they have become used to the filth and heaps of waste lying around. The blocked drains and heaps of garbage provide breeding and feeding ground for mosquitoes, flies and rodents. Collectively these can cause diarrhea, malaria and several other infectious diseases.

During rainy season the condition becomes worst. Most of the chocked nullahs and drains start overflowing, spilling the garbage on the roads and streets causing great inconvenience to general public and creating health problems. At collection points and dumping ground sometimes people of the locality due to lack of awareness burn the waste to get rid of it. Open burning of garbage poses health risks to those exposed directly to the smoke. It especially affects people with sensitive respiratory systems, as well as children and the elderly. In the short term, exposure to smoke can cause headaches, nausea, and rashes. Over time, it can increase the risk of developing heart disease. Some of the pollutants contained in the smoke from open burning of garbage can include:

- Dioxins
- Furans
- Arsenic
- Mercury
- PCBs
- Lead
- Carbon monoxide
- Nitrogen oxides
- Sulphur oxides
- Hydrochloric acid
- Ashes left after burning the garbage mix with air and cause air pollution

PROBLEMS FACED BY PEOPLE ENGAGED IN GARBAGE DISPOSAL

Safai karamcharies engaged in garbage collection are not provided with necessary protective devices like gloves, gumboots, masks and proper uniform. They are exposed to unhygienic conditions and are subjected to several health hazards.

Fig. 8.19: **Open Burning of Garbage**

***Fig. 8.20 (a, b, c, d)*: Pictures Showing Safai Karamcharies Working in Unhygienic Conditions without Necessary Protective Devices like Gloves, Gumboots, Masks and Proper Uniform**

During the process of transport of garbage from collection points to the dumping grounds and then to the trenches the waste is carried openly in tractors and trolleys, which are overloaded with garbage. Most of these waste spills from the trucks on the road making roads dirty and causing lots of inconvenience for the pedestrians, producing foul smell and polluting the environment.

Fig. 8.21: **Waste being Carried in Overloaded Trucks and Garbage Spilling on Road**

Garbage is dumped at collection points, dumping grounds and trenches without being sorted into biodegradable and non-biodegradable waste. The garbage dumped on trenching grounds is potential source of many health hazard and poses grave threat to local environment. Methane is formed by decomposition of organic matter in dump yards, which has 24 times more global warming potential than that of CO_2.

Fig. 8.22: **Trenching Grounds**

THE RAG PICKERS

The sorting of the garbage is done neither by safai karamcharies nor at the sources. There is another section of people called the rag pickers who serve the purpose of sorting out different contents of the garbage. They play a vital role for the city. They can be considered as invisible environmentalists. But unfortunately they are usually neglected by the -society. Though they do it to earn their livelihood. They play the role of Silent environmentalists. They may not be themselves aware of it or may not even understand the term, but they play a significant role in the waste disposal.

Every morning these rag pickers are seen on the streets of the city carrying rags on their shoulder collecting the plastic and other harmful non biodegradable waste from the garbage. This way they do an important work of sorting out of garbage. If they will not perform their job the garbage would be left without being sorted out. By collecting household garbage they reduce the city's solid waste management cost, provide a recycling system where none would exist otherwise and reduce the amount of waste which ends up in landfills. Inspite of their significant role their condition is quite pathetic. They are denied of all their basic entitlements, rather they remain unrecognized by the society. Like safai karamcharies they work in unhygienic conditions and are exposed to intense health risks such as musculo-skeletal problems, respiratory and gastro-intestinal ailments apart from nicks and cuts and animal bites as they jostle to collect, sort and sell trash.

Fig. 8.23: **The Rag Pickers Collecting the Waste**

PHERIWALAS

Besides rag pickers there is another category of people who also play an important role in sorting out non biodegradable waste. They are pheriwalas, who go from mohallah to mohallah and purchase items like plastic bags, bottles, bones, metals, glass, paper etc. In a way they provide incentive to the people to keep such items separately to be sold out to pheriwalas.

Fig. 8.24: **Pheriwala Collecting the Waste**

SUGGESTIONS FOR GARBAGE MANAGEMENT

Since the garbage is dumped without getting sorted into biodegradable and non-biodegradable wastes. Separate bins should be used at the sources like households and shops etc.

Most people of the city are poor and illiterate so these bins should be provided by the government or municipal board. And the colour of the bins should vary according to the type of garbage they are meant for, *viz.*:

- Green for Fruits vegetables and other kitchen leftovers.
- Red for metal,glass, plastic waste.
- Blue for paper waste.

Fig. 8.25: **Different Colour Bins to Collect Different Wastes**

The safai karamcharies and rag pickers who play a great role in garbage disposal, their conditions of working should be improved. They should be provided with gloves, shoes, masks, and proper cleaning facilities. Their status should be raised in the society and they should be made proud of the work they do. Schemes should be made for their health insurance, education and their income status should be raised. Trucks that carry garbage should be covered to prevent garbage from spilling on the ground and polluting the environment.

Fig. 8.26: **Covered Trucks to Prevent Garbage from Spilling**

SOLID WASTE MANAGEMENT PROJECT IN RAMPUR

During our study we found that at one of the trenching grounds an old signboard is still installed indicating that the site is meant for the solid waste management project. However on inquiry it was learnt that the scheme of solid waste management has been shifted to another place called "Tikat ganj", and even the local people are opposing the project.

Fig. 8.27: **Signboard Indicating Solid Waste Management Project**

RECYCLING PLANTS

Plants for recycling of garbage should be installed by the government. There are various recycling techniques that can be helpful in disposal of garbage in environmental friendly way. These recycling plants will not only be helpful in garbage disposal but will also provide employment to a large number of people. Some of the plants that can be established for this purpose are following:

RECYCLING AT INDUSTRIAL LEVEL

Vermiculture

Vermiculture appears to be an innovative sustainable technology for waste management, which holds a promising future in solid waste management. It is the process of culturing worms to decompose organic food waste, and turning waste into nutrient rich material capable of supplying necessary nutrients to help plant growth. Vermiculture may supply an opportunity for employment.

From Waste to Energy

Another plan that can help in garbage management is conversion of waste to energy. Energy from waste offers recovery of energy by conversion of non-recyclable materials through various processes including thermal and non-thermal technologies. Independent studies and scientific evidence around the world have concluded that the energy that is produced in the form of electricity, heat or fuel is clean and renewable energy, with reduced carbon emissions and minimal environmental impact than any other form of energy.

Recycling at Individual Level

Not only at industrial level but people should be trained and encouraged to practice recycling techniques at home. Following are the recycling methods that we can use at home.

Compositing

Composting is the most sustainable option for managing organic waste. It can be easily done at home and good for the environment. Compost is the product resulting from the controlled biological decomposition of organic material that has been sanitized through the generation of heat and stabilized to the point that it is beneficial to plant growth. We can easily convert organic waste into nutrient-rich humus which fuels plant growth and restores vitality to depleted soil.

Garbage Enzyme (Housewhold Cleanser)

Fruit and vegetable scraps can be used for making our own household cleanser, which can be used for cleaning purpose. The method is as following:

- 1 Part molasses
- three parts veggie/fruit peels
- 10 Parts water

Keep the above ingredients in air tight container shake it and let it ferment. And garbage enzyme will be ready in 3 months then filter it and use it as a household cleanser.

Fig. 8.28: **Garbage Enzyme**

Awareness among people

People should be made aware about the hazards of the garbage and should be encouraged for correct disposal of garbage. i.e. *RECYCLING, REUSE & REDUCE* Should be encouraged among the people. Pamphlets, street shows, slogans should be used to generate awareness and to encourage people to practice proper garbage disposal. Since most people are aware but they do not practice it so people should be encouraged to bring that awareness into practice. Children should be made aware, trained and encouraged at early age through books and school plays at schools. NGO's and committees should be made by the people of every mohallah for cleanliness and sanitation. Cooperation between common man and municipal board is essential to keep the city clean.

CONCLUSION

The findings of our study can be summarized as follows:

- Rampur Municipal board is grappling with problem of garbage management in the old hackneyed manner and the success in tackling the problem is only partial.
- Garbage is shifted from one point to another. Shifting garbage from one point to another is not the solution of the problem. Man power or the number of safai karamcharies is much below the prescribed norm. Safai Karamcharis remain neglected. They are not provided even with basic facilities. Drains and nullahs quite often get choked.
- Polythene bags and such other items are the major cause of choking the drainage system. At present the drainage of the city is being redesigned and reconstructed for improvement.
- Lack of people's participation in cleaning of the city is very much evident. The problem is quite enormous which requires serious efforts on larger scale and on modern scientific lines.
- The safai karamcharies must be inspired with greater zeal to do their job well. They should be provided with protective accessories. Their socioeconomic conditions must be improved.
- Common citizens must be actively involved in the cleanliness efforts through launching cleanliness drives from time to time. Solid waste management plant must be installed at the earliest.

REFRENCES

1. http://www.authorstream.com/Presentation/hemantraakh-2100085-garbage-disposal-hugechallenge-india
2. http://www.livestrong.com/article/124375-effects-improper-garbage-disposal
3. http://www.dairynet.com/energy_resources/landfill.php
4. http://urbanext.illinois.edu/compost/process.cfm
5. http://www.wikihow.com/Manage-Your-Home-Waste
6. Krieth Frank 1994 Hand book of solid waste management
7. http://commercemagnj.com/thinking-outside-the-landfill-how-waste-to-energy-can-provide-a-greener-solution-to-garbage-disposal/
8. http://burningman.org/event/preparation/leaving-no-trace/
9. http://www.scientificamerican.com/article/does-burning-garbage-to-produce-energy-make-sense/
10. http://www.vermico.com/vermicomposting-technology-for-waste-management-agriculture-an-executive-summary/
11. Energy Generation from Municipal Solid Waste "The Hindu" (12.06.2013) pp.16.
12. http://www.pollutionpollution.com/2012/07/about-garbage-pollution

***Pages:* 100-107**

WASTE MANAGEMENT AND ENVIRONMENTAL HEALTH

***Edited by:* Dr. B. Tabassum; Dr. Priya Bajaj & Dr. Pawan Kumar 'Bharti'**

ISBN: 978-93-5056-777-7

***Edition:* 2016**

***Published by:* Discovery Publishing House Pvt. Ltd., New Delhi (India)**

Electronic Waste
A Threat to Biodiversity

Sara Sayeed[1] and Shahla Nusrat Qidwai[2]

ABSTRACT

Over the recent past, the global market of electrical and electronic waste (e-waste; WEE) has grown exponentially, and is currently the largest growing waste stream. On the other hand the lifespan of these products has become increasingly shorter. This article delineates, reviews and explores the sources, volumes and flows of e-wastes and the risk they pose to the environment and people surrounding it. Most of these products are ending up in rubbish dumps and recycling centers, obsolete and dumped electronic gadgets are posing a new challenge to policy makers. The purpose of this article is to provide a review of the e-waste problem and to put forward possible solutions against their risk.

[1]Department of Electronics and Computer Engineering, Integral University, Lucknow (UP).

[2]Department of Chemistry, Govt. Raza PG College, Rampur (UP).

Corresponding Author: Dr. Shahla Nusrat Qidwai, Department of Chemistry, Govt. Raza PG College, Rampur (UP) - 244 901, *Email:* sara11dmite@gmail.com, *Mob.:* +91 9412151677

INTRODUCTION

Over the past two decades, the global market of electrical and electronic equipment continues to grow exponentially in developed as well as developing countries, while the lifespan of these products have become shorter and shorter. Thereby, business as well as waste management officials are facing a new challenge and e-waste or waste electrical and electronic equipment (WEE) is receiving considerable amount of attention from policy makers.

E-waste is any refuse created by discarded electronic devices and components as well as substances involved in their manufacturing. There is no standard definition of e-waste, but according to Organization for Economic Co-operation and Development (OECD)

"e-Waste is the term used to describe old, end-of-life or discarded appliances using electricity."

The most widely accepted definition of e-waste is as per European Commission Directive 2002/96/EC-

"electrical or electronic equipment, which is waste including all components, subassemblies and consumables, which are part of the product at the time of discarding".

The differences in definitions of what constitutes e-waste have the potential to create disparities in both the quantification of e-waste generation and the identification of e-waste flows. The e-wastes include computers, DVD's, consumer electronics, fridges, CRT's, computer peripheral, stereo equipments, VCR's etc which have been disposed of by their users.

It has been predicted that the number of electrical and electronic devices will continue to increase on the global scale and will be used in numbers in daily objects that are necessities of life. Consequently, the volume of WEE grows rapidly every year and is also believed to be one of the most critical waste disposal issues of the twenty-first century. United Nation University estimates that 20 to 50 tons of e-Waste is being generated per year worldwide. Compared to conventional municipal wastes, certain components of electronic products contain toxic substances, which can generate a threat to the environment as well as to human health. For instance, television and computer monitors normally contain hazardous materials such as lead, mercury, and cadmium, while nickel, beryllium, and zinc can often be found in circuit boards. Due to the presence of these substances, recycling and disposal of e-Waste becomes an important issue.

Many of us are unaware of the negative impact of the rapidly increasing use of computers, monitors, and televisions. The rapidly increasing WEE mass flow, combined with the trend towards embedded electronics, makes WEE an emerging risk for society. When these products are placed in landfills or incinerated, they pose serious health risks due to the hazardous materials they contain. The improper disposal of electronic products leads to the possibility of damaging the environment and elevates risk of cancer and developmental and neurological disorders. An additional aspect of e-waste is that the loss of sensitive personal information which could even give rise to security problems.

GLOBAL SIGNIFICANCE, ISSUES AND FLOW OF E-WASTE

The cost of recycling e-Waste exceeds the revenue recovered from materials especially in countries with strict environment regulations. Therefore, e-Waste mostly ends up dumped in countries where environmental standards are low or nonexistent and working conditions are poor. The term "bridging the digital divide" is used when old WEE are exported to developing countries. They are often labeled as "second-hand goods" since export of reusable goods is allowed. Recycling and disposal of e-Waste are also growing in regions beyond Asia, particularly in certain African countries. Recently, a report from Toxics Link reveals that 70 percent of WEE disposed in New Delhi of India was imported from developed countries. Alarming levels of dioxin compounds in samples of breast milk, placenta and hair, linked to cancer, developmental defects, and other health problems are due to improper disposal of electronic products. e-Waste exports large amounts of digital discards that are transported internationally from various industrialized countries to certain destinations where there are lower environmental standards and working conditions. This make processing e-Waste more profitable in these countries.

The main issues posed by e-waste are as following:

- **High volumes:** High volumes are generated due to the rapid obsolescence of gadgets combined with the high demand for new technology (Basel Action Network; BAN).
- **Toxic design:** E-waste is classified as hazardous waste having adverse health and environmental implications. Approximately 40 per cent of the heavy metals found in landfills come from electronic waste (Montrose, 2011).
- **Poor design and complexity:** E-waste imposes many challenges on the recycling industry as it contains many different materials that are

mixed, bolted, screwed, snapped, glued or soldered together. Toxic materials are attached to non-toxic materials, which makes separation of materials for reclamation difficult. Hence, responsible recycling requires intensive labour and/or sophisticated and costly technologies that safely separate material.

- **Labour issues:** These include occupational exposures, informal sector domination causing health and environmental problems, lack of labour standards and rights.
- **Financial incentives:** In general, there is not enough value in most e-waste to cover the costs of managing it in a responsible way. However, in line with EPR policies, new opportunities can be realized with the rise in the price of many of the materials in electronics, such as gold and copper.
- **Lack of regulation:** Many nations either lack adequate regulations applying to this relatively new waste stream, or lack effective enforcement of new e-waste regulations.

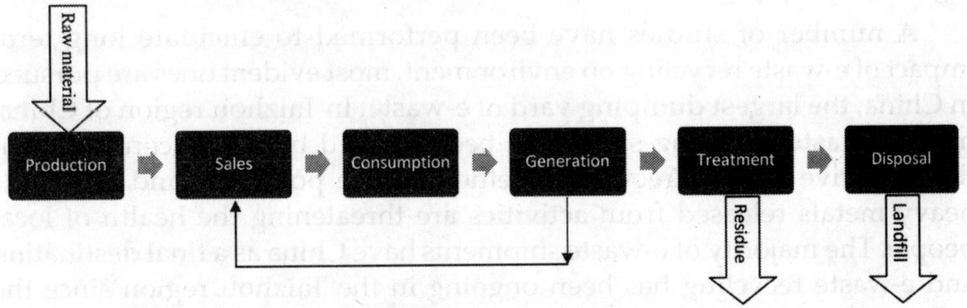

Fig. 9.1: **Life Cycle of e-Waste**

RISK OF E-WASTES TO HUMAN HEALTH AND ENVIRONMENT

E-waste is a complex and difficult form of waste to recycle, and problems such as elevated concentrations of heavy metals in the air have even been found. Workers and local residents are exposed to toxic chemicals through inhalation, dust ingestion, dermal exposure and oral intake. It is evident from several studies in Ghana, China that the rudimentary recycling techniques coupled with the amounts of e-waste processed have already resulted in adverse environmental and human health impacts, including contaminated soil and surface water

A particular hazard associated with the disassembly stage is the possibility of accidental release and spillage of hazardous substances upon breakage of the shell, such as mercury, which is found within light sources as well as switches. CRTs present the risk of implosion due to the vacuum inside the tubes and inhalation hazard due to phosphor coating on the inner side of the glass. The dusts and the surrounding ambient air may pose an inhalation hazard (e.g. polycyclic aromatic hydrocarbons (PAHs) and dermal exposure hazard to workers, as well as the risk of environmental contamination. Toxins are also transmitted orally via people's hands when eating. Atmospheric pollution due to burning and dismantling activities seems to be the main cause of occupational and secondary exposure. Food chain also gets contaminated as toxins gets accumulated in agricultural lands and be available for up take by grazing livestock. Many chemicals have a slow metabolic rate in animals, and may bio-accumulate in tissues and be excreted in edible products such as eggs and milk.

Exposure of children and pregnant women to lead, mercury, cadmium and other heavy metals can cause serious and irreversible neurological damage and threaten the development of the child. They often suffer from poor labour conditions and face various risks and hazards, varying from occupational accidents to heavy metal and chemical poisoning, and ergonomic and psychosocial problems.

A number of studies have been performed to elucidate long term impact of e-waste recycling on environment, most evident ones are pursued in China, the largest dumping yard of e-waste. In Taizhou region of China, many e-waste recycling sites have been studied based on concerns that the primitive e-waste recycling methods cause pollution, and that toxic heavy metals released from activities are threatening the health of local people. The majority of e-waste shipments have China as a final destination and e-waste recycling has been ongoing in the Taizhou region since the 1970s. In this region, the majority of the dismantling and recovery processes are usually carried out in small household workshops in rural villages, where most of the residents are directly or indirectly involved in e-waste related activities (Wang et al., 2011).

In the e-waste recycling centers around Luqiao and Wenling, researchers studied the impact of heavy metals in 349 people and compared results with a control group of 118 people. Questionnaire surveys for risk factors were also performed and analyzed. It was found that urinary levels of lead, cadmium, manganese, copper, and zinc were considerably elevated. Results of the study indicated that the levels of urinary cadmium in both workers and people living in the area were significantly higher than in the control group. The primitive e-waste recycling activities are therefore the cause of the changes of urinary heavy metal levels and indicate increased health risk for those permanently working in e-waste recycling

(Wang *et al.*, 2011). In the same region, Zhao and others studied possible dual pollution of PCBs and PBDEs. This was because the recycling of e-waste in Luqiao began in the late 1970s, where a large number of PCBs-containing transformers and capacitors were treated, whereas recycling of e-waste in Wenling began in the late 1990s, where various PBDEs-containing e-wastes were disassembled. Because Luqiao is 25 km away from Wenling, it was suggested that a "cocktail effect" of PCBs and PBDEs could be occurring in the human body within the region. Blood samples were collected from the two e-waste recycling sites and presented dual body burdens of PCBs and PBDEs at high levels. It is suggested that dual burdens of PCBs and PBDEs at such high levels pose health risk for local residents. This raises concerns about human health risk of dual exposure in relation to developmental neurotoxicity, high cancer risk and thyroid-disrupting activities deficits (Zhao et al., 2010)

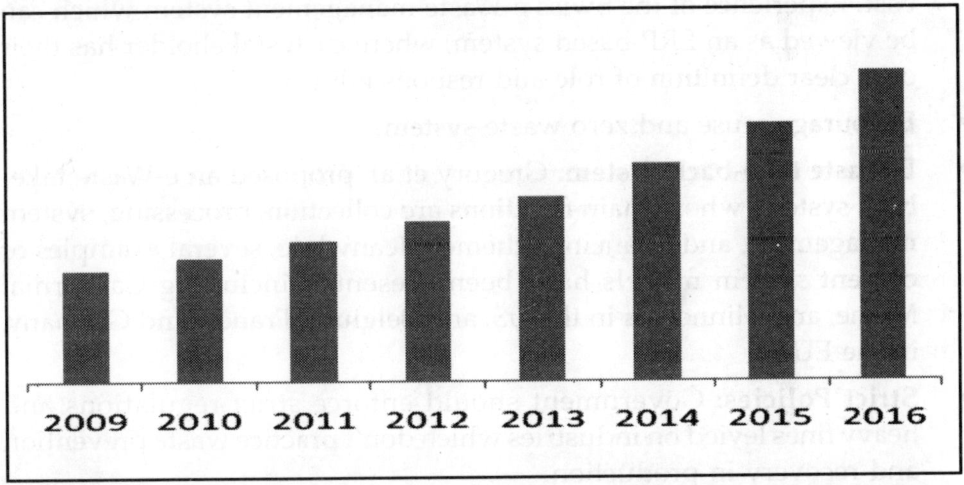

Annual Urinary Cadmium Level in Workers Around Luqiao and Wenling

POSSIBLE SOLUTIONS AND CHALLENGES

There should be ways through which sustainable development could be outreached. e-waste is a significant cross-cutting issue with global significance and it therefore requires cross-sectoral implementation. Following steps could be considered significantly to resolve the risk factors of e-wastes:

- **Creation of Green Jobs:** Workers in green jobs help to recycle and repurpose electronics that could otherwise end up in landfills or, worse, as e-waste in developing nations. In addition, the revenue generated from recycled computer equipment supports training programmes, employment placement services and other community-based programmes for people who have disabilities, lack education or job experience.

- **The Mantra of 3R's:** "Reduce, Reuse and Recycle" should be practiced and taken into account by each one of us.
- **The design:** The design should be sustainable such that:
  - (a) Renewable materials should be used e.g. solar computers.
  - (b) Rethink the product design i.e. efforts should be made to design a product with fewer amount of hazardous components.
- **Consumer awareness efforts** should be outraged like e-Cycle which is the first mobile buyback and recycling company, Best Buy and staples etc. which also accepts electronic items for recycling at no additional cost. Experience of the Swiss e-Waste management system which can be viewed as an ERP-based system, where each stakeholder has their own clear definition of role and responsibilities.
- Encourage reuse and zero waste system.
- **E-Waste take-back system:** Gregory et al. proposed an e-Waste take-back system, whose main functions are collection, processing, system management, and financing scheme. Meanwhile, several examples of current system models have been presented including California, Maine, and Minnesota in the US, and Belgium, France, and Germany, in the EU.
- **Strict Policies:** Government should enforce strict regulations and heavy fines levied on industries which don't practice waste prevention and recovery in production.
- **Research and Development:** Government should encourage research and development in waste management, disposal and environmental monitoring. And should support NGO's financially who are looking after this like Saahas and EWA, in Bangalore.

CONCLUSION

E-waste has boomed over from last few decades. And there should be an urgent check on it otherwise our environment will be severely affected. Recycling is the key to reduce the e-Waste. Recycling has environmental benefits at every stage in the life cycle of a WEE —from the raw material from which it is made to its final method of disposal. Aside from reducing greenhouse gas emissions, which contribute to global warming, recycling also reduces air and water pollution associated with making new products.

The solution to the e-waste problem is not simply the banning of trans-boundary movements of e-waste, as domestic generation accounts for a significant proportion of e-waste in all countries. It is important to recognize that implementing a high-tech, capital-intensive recycling process will not be appropriate in every country or region. Effective regulation must be combined with incentives for recyclers in the informal sector not to engage in destructive processes. Cheap, safe and simple processing methods for introduction into the informal sector are currently lacking; hence, it is necessary to create a financial incentive for recyclers operating in the informal sector to deliver recovered parts to central collection sites rather than process them themselves. By utilizing used, unwanted, or obsolete materials as industrial feedstock or for new materials or products, we can do our part to make recycling work.

REFERENCES

1. Babu, B.R.; Parande, A.K.; Basha, C.A. 2007. "Electrical and Electronic Waste: A Global Environmental Problem", in Waste Management and Research, Vol. 25, pp. 307-318.
2. C. Davis, "Why is Electronic Waste a Problem? Earthtrends," 2006.
3. Chi, X. 2011. "Informal Electronic Waste Recycling: A Sector Review with special focus on China", in Waste Management, Vol. 31, No. 4, p. 731-742.
4. Defining and Categorization of Wastes via the Regulations". IT Green Greenpeace, Basel Action Network.
5. Electronic waste-en.wikipedia.org/wiki/Electronic_waste, E-waste guide info.
6. Facts and Figures on E-Waste and Recycling.
7. J. Gregory, F. Magalini, R. Kuehr, and J. Huisman, "E-waste take-back System Design and Policy Approaches," Solving the e-Waste Problem (StEP), White Paper, 2009.
8. M. Khurrum S. Bhutta, Adnan Omar, and Xiaozhe Yang "Electronic Waste: A Growing Concern in Today's Environment"
9. Science Daily, "Recycling of e-waste in China may Expose Mothers, Infants to High Dioxin Levels, Science News, 2007.
10. United Nations Environment Programme (UNEP) Reducing Risk from Mercury.
11. A Global Impact of e-waste, www.ilo.org, wcms_196105.
12. http://earthtrends.wri.org/updates/node/130.
13. http://www.electronicstakeback.com/resources/facts-and-figures/
14. http://ewasteguide.info/
15. http://www.unep.org/hazardous substances.

***Pages:* 108-116**

WASTE MANAGEMENT AND ENVIRONMENTAL HEALTH
***Edited by:* Dr. B. Tabassum; Dr. Priya Bajaj & Dr. Pawan Kumar 'Bharti'**
ISBN: 978-93-5056-777-7
***Edition:* 2016**
***Published by:* Discovery Publishing House Pvt. Ltd., New Delhi (India)**

Waste Management in School and Role of Students

Ahsan Ali

INTRODUCTION

Environmental problem is a global concern, without discrimination of boundaries. We are born from the environment, we return to the it and we are sustained by the environment. Hence the environment in which we live is very important and it directly affects our lives. It is said that man is the product of his environment. Around the world; efforts are being made to make people aware about environmental protection.

One of the main causes of environmental degradation is improper management in the disposal of solid waste. It is a major cause of pollution and outbreak of diseases in many parts of the world. There is no permanent solution for environmental problems, only thing we can reduce and control

Department of Education, Teerthanker Mahaveer University, Moradabad

Corresponding Author: Ahsan Ali, C/o Saeed-ur-Rehman, Angoori Bagh, Near Police Chawki Rajjad, Rampur (UP) - 244 901, *Email:* aliahsanali819@gmail.com, *Mob.*: +91 -9719135650

waste generation by proper awareness and practice. Proper management of the waste generated is most important in this matter. Waste management is a science that addresses the logistics, environmental impact, social responsibility and cost of an organizations' waste disposal.

Solid Waste Management (SWM) has 3 basic components namely collection, transportation and disposal. Comprehensive solid waste management incorporates a diverse range of activities including reduction, recycling, segregation, modification, treatment and disposal which have varying levels of sophistication (Zagozewski *et al*, 2011). The objective of SWM is to reduce the quantity of solid waste disposed off on land by recovery of materials and energy from solid waste in a cost effective and environmental friendly manner (MF, 2009). It is estimated that 1, 60000 MT (Metric Tonne) of municipal solid waste is generated daily in India. According to the 2001 census, per capita waste generation in India is 0.5 Kg/day (Vinod & Venugopal, 2010). Waste management activities generate potential environmental benefits if managed properly (Gentil et al, 2009). There has been hardly any effort in the past to create community awareness, either about the likely perils due to poor waste management or the simple steps that every citizen can take. This could have helped in reducing waste generation and promote effective waste management. But this scenario has changed. Nowadays more and more people are taking interest in environmental issues, as they have started to experience the ill-effects of ecological issues. Now environmental education is welcomed by all categories of people. It is an attempt to reorient education so that environmental competence is restored as one of its basic aims along with personal and social competence (Shobeiri et al, 2007). Environmental problems are many. It is mounting high with new problems like disposal of e-waste. E-waste is a collective terminology for the entire stream of electronic equipment such as TV, refrigerators, telephones, air conditioners, computers, mobile phones etc. that has reached its End of Life (EOL) for its current user. Such devices are generally considered toxic when disassembled or incinerated and are typically targeted for hazardous disposal or are slated for necessary recovery and reuse (MF, 2009).

One of the greatest challenges facing developing countries is the unhealthy disposal of solid waste which resulted from human activities of development and survival (Onibokun, 1999; Osinowo, 2001; Joseph, 2006; Longe & William, 2006; Kofoworola, 2007). It is a problem recognized by all nations at the 1992 Conference on Environment and Development, and regarded as a major barrier in the path towards sustainability (UNCED, 1992).

The office that is responsible for the oversight and management of solid waste is the likely candidate to be responsible for the waste reduction, reuse, recycling and composting. Your procurement office should be responsible for the purchasing of recycled products and packaging. All directives concerning this programme need to come out of the Superintendent or Principal. If everyone knows that upper management is behind this programme you will have better participation. But everyone should be involved, students, faculty, custodial staff, office staff, each and everyone.

MEANING OF WASTE

Wastes are those items that we (individuals, offices, schools, industries, hospitals) don't need and discard. Sometimes there are things we have that the law requires us to discard because they can be harmful. Waste comes in infinite sizes-some can be as small as an old toothbrush, or as large as the body of a school bus.

Everyone creates waste, although some people are very environmentally conscious and create very little. Likewise, some countries do a very good job creating less waste and managing the rest. Others are pretty horrible and have created huge environmental problems for the people and animals living there.

All over the world, communities handle their waste or trash differently. Some common methods of managing their waste include land filling, recycling and composting. Other communities strongly embark on waste reduction and litter prevention/control aimed at reducing the production of waste in the first place. Some communities also engage in waste-to-energy plants and hazardous waste disposal programmes.

WASTE MANAGEMENT IN SCHOOLS

Managing is an important aspect of human survival to:

- Ensure a safe and healthy work environment for employees, students and visitors.
- Protect the environment by using sound principles of handling, treatment, storage and disposal of hazardous waste.
- Minimise the generation as well as cost of handling and disposing of hazardous materials.
- To reduce the amount of waste going into landfill or to incineration.

The school will take reasonable steps to minimize the waste it produces. Where there are materials that are no longer required the following options will be considered:

- **Reduce:** Avoid the need to discard materials in general.
- **Re-use:** Pass on equipment to others before disposing of it.
- **Recycle:** Segregation of materials for recycling to reduce the waste at the school.

This plan establishes a way to address the global solid waste problem. The hierarchy is as follows:

- First, to reduce the amount of solid waste generated;
- Second, to reuse material for the purpose for which it was originally intended or to recycle material that cannot be reused;
- Third, to recover, in an environmentally acceptable manner, energy from solid waste that cannot be economically and technically reused or recycled; and
- Fourth, to dispose of solid waste that is not being reused, recycled or from which energy is not being recovered, by land burial or other methods approved by the DEC.

TO REDUCE WASTE

Although recycling is an important part of any waste management strategy, the greatest environmental benefits are achieved through source reduction and reuse. Consider a simple example; we can reduce trash disposal and save raw materials if we collect plastic grocery bags for recycling and incorporate them into a new product such as plastic lumber. However, a better option would be to take no bag at all, as no natural resources or energy are used to first produce,

Then collect and reprocess disposable bags. Using a reusable canvas or string bag would have similar environmental benefits as the bag could replace thousands of disposable bags over its useful life. Any organization reviewing their waste management strategy should first consider ways to reduce waste and incorporate reusable products to achieve the maximum benefit to the environment. Your efforts may provide the additional benefit of saving money as well. Remember, even small changes can make a big difference. Following efforts may be considered in this reference:

- Make double-sided copies whenever possible. This can dramatically reduce your paper usage.

- Instead of making individual copies for everyone, use a routing slip when circulating information to staff, or post notices on a bulletin board. Better yet, an electronic bulletin board.
- Use reusable envelopes for interoffice mail.
- If applicable, use electronic mail instead of making hard copies of all communications.
- If possible, limit the number of subscriptions to periodicals and share them. This will reduce both trash and subscription costs.
- Encourage the reuse of office supplies, i.e. paper clips, rubber bands and brass fasteners, etc.
- Use scrap paper for messages and make your own scrap pads.
- Require suppliers who deliver products on pallets or in metal drums to take them back.
- Have your cafeteria switch to reusable utensils and dishes instead of throwaways whenever possible. Investigate the possibility of switching to refillable containers for milk and juice.
- Purchase reusable and washable cleaning cloths, aprons, tablecloths, etc., rather than single-use disposable products.
- Buy institutional sizes of "green" cleaning supplies, food products, beverages, etc.
- Buy recycled content paper products, like, copier paper, paper towels, napkins, toilet paper.

TO REUSE WASTE

You may also want to incorporate reuse into special projects or activities at the school. A few examples of this type of project are listed. Hold a "SWAP DAY". Have student bring in items from home to swap with other children. (Of course parental permission will be needed.) You may want to limit the types of items that can be brought in to items such as books or small toys to facilitate "even trading". This can be part of a history lesson in the development of trade and monetary systems. Following small tips may accelerate the process of reuse:

- Collect other reusable such as clothing for local charities.
- Maintain a free listing service of used musical instruments and sporting equipment in your school newsletter. Parents will appreciate this effort. It may encourage some children to try an activity that their family might not be able to otherwise afford.

- Incorporate the use of reusable into your art programme. Host a sculpture contest in which the children make their creations from items that would have been recycled or thrown away. This can be fun even without the added incentive of a contest.
- Incorporate the use of reusable into your science programme by hosting an inventor fair. Have the children design some machine or other contraption from found items. You will be amazed at what the children come up with!
- Establish a bird feeding/observation area with feeders made from containers that have already been used once for another purpose such as milk jugs, paper milk cartons, soda bottles, etc. Establish a site where these feeders can stay for an extended period of time. Allow the children some observation time to record which birds frequent the different feeders.

TO RECYCLE WASTE

All schools must recycle what is mandated in their community. A basic recycling programme would include paper, metal, glass, and plastic, but there is much more to consider. The following provides you with information on the basic recyclables and other recyclables to consider. The best way to develop a recycling programme is to conduct a waste audit to see what materials you generate and where they come from.

RECYCLABLE MATERIALS

1. Paper

Paper constitutes the largest single component of the municipal waste stream - over 1/3 by weight. Markets exist for many types of waste paper. Remember, collecting paper for recycling is only half of the cycle. You need to have a proactive purchasing programme to buy paper made from post-consumer recycled materials. Recycled paper is available in all types with quality and pricing comparable to paper made from "virgin" raw materials. The four categories of paper that are most relevant to school recycling programmes are:

- **High-grade white office paper** includes **white** typing, writing, and copy paper, white scratch paper, index cards and computer paper.
- **Mixed office paper** is recovered from offices and schools in an unsorted but clean form, and usually includes white, colored, glossy, junk mail and magazines.

- **Corrugated cardboard** is used to ship merchandise. For maximum value, Contaminants such as polystyrene, packing materials, plastic-coated cartons and other debris should be removed.
- **Old newspapers** (can include telephone books) should be kept clean and dry.

Paper markets fluctuate with supply and demand. When the supply of paper is plentiful, markets retain suppliers of high quality materials who can guarantee large tonnages of paper free of contaminants. Therefore, it is advisable to design your programme to maximize both quality and quantity of the waste paper collected.

2. **Glass, Plastic & Metal:**

   All schools should have a programme to recycle all plastic, glass & metal food and beverage containers. This includes both the containers generated during food preparation as well as those generated by vending machines, lunches brought to school, etc. Since these items are also collected in much larger quantities from homes in every community, your school may want to use the same collection and processing system that serves local residents.

3. Disks (3.5)
4. Smoke Detectors
5. CD's
6. Styrofoam Peanuts (reused)
7. Ink Jet Cartridges
8. Toner & Printer Cartridges
9. Fluorescent Lights and Ballasts
10. Typed Envelopes

PROMOTION OF WASTE MANAGEMENT IN SCHOOLS

An ongoing educational programme is required to assure your programme's continued success. When you first kick off the recycling programme, reminders to recycle should be prominently posted throughout the building, in cafeterias, lounges, conference area, elevators, stairwells, on bulletin boards, etc. Following educational tools may help you in this process:

1. Slogans and Logos

You may want to develop a slogan or logo for your recycling programme. A poster campaign specifically developed for your programme will promote interest and participation. Your staff and students will be able to identify with it and interest will be stimulated.

2. Educational Pamphlets

In addition to a kick-off memo, you may want to develop an educational pamphlet or brochure. Given to all the employees, it can become a useful reminder of your programme. It can also be used for good public relations, if shared with other companies or schools.

3. Social Media

Posting these materials on your website or through social media outlets are a great waste reduction measure.

4. Publicity

Your recycling programme may be of interest to the community. Do not hesitate to contact local TV, radio stations and newspapers. They may like the opportunity to report on your recycling efforts.

5. Status Reports

Status reports on the success of your recycling programme should be included on a regular basis to staff and students. Use statistics give them an idea of how much has been saved by recycling. Everyone likes feedback on how they are doing.

6. Orientation

Be sure to include information on your recycling programme as part of new employee or student.

CONCLUSION

The impact of current and historical waste disposal practices on the environment and human health has yet to be adequately addressed. Solid waste disposal has been identified as a major environmental threat. Overtime waste disposal evolved to weekly pick-up of un-segregated garbage with waste disposal and open trash burning in a dump site, Dump site locations and open trash burning in/around the school premises are identified as significant health issues related to waste disposal practices. This review raises issues of inequity in the management of waste in schools.

It highlights the need for long-term sustainable funding to support community-based waste disposal and management strategies and the development of centered and delivered educational programmes to encourage the adoption and implementation of waste reduction, reutilization and recycling activities in schools.

REFERENCES

1. http://www.dec.ny.gov/docs/materials_minerals_pdf/schoolhb.pdf. A School Waste Reduction, Reuse, Recycling, Composting & Buy Recycled Resource Book.
2. http://www.dnr.wi.gov/files/pdf/pubs/wa/wa1561.pdf. Recycling and Waste Reduction: A Guide For schools.
2. http://www.en.wikipedia.org/wiki/waste management/Waste Management
3. http://www.epa.gov/osw/education/toolkit.html Tools to Reduce Waste in School
4. http://www.eschooltoday.com/waste...../Waste Management-tips-for-kids.html. Waste Management- e-school Today.
5. http://www.Schoolsanitation.com/pdf/Waste-Management-in-schools.pdf. Solid Waste Management in School"
6. http://www.wm.com/enterprise/k-12-education/ School Recycling & Waste Disposal/Waste Management.
7. Vivek et al., (2013) Awareness, Attitude and Practice of School Students Towards Household Waste management. Journal of Environment; 2 (6): 147-150.
8. Zagozewski R., Ian Judd-Henrey, Suzie Nilson and Lalita Bharadwaj (2011) Perspectives on Past and Present Waste Disposal Practices: A Community-Based Participatory Research Project in Three Saskatchewan First Nations Communities. *Environmental Health Insights*; 5: 9-20.

Pages: 117-124

WASTE MANAGEMENT AND ENVIRONMENTAL HEALTH

Edited by: **Dr. B. Tabassum; Dr. Priya Bajaj & Dr. Pawan Kumar 'Bharti'**

ISBN: 978-93-5056-777-7

Edition: **2016**

Published by: **Discovery Publishing House Pvt. Ltd., New Delhi (India)**

Sanitation in India
Health and Environmental Issue

Sanjiv Kumar

INTRODUCTION

India is still lagging far behind many countries in the field of environmental sanitation. The unsanitary conditions are appalling in India and need a great sanitary awakening. Improvement in sanitation requires newer strategies and targeted interventions with follow-up evaluation. The need of the hour is to identify the existing system of environmental sanitation with respect to its structure and functioning and to prioritize the control strategies according to the need of the country. These priorities are particularly important because of issue of water constraints, environment-related health problems, rapid population growth, inequitable distribution of water resources, issues related to administrative problems, urbanization and industrialization, migration of population, and rapid economic growth.

B.Ed. Department, Govt. Raza P.G. College, Rampur.

Corresponding Author: Dr. Sanjiv Kumar, Department of B. Ed., Govt. Raza P G College, Rampur (UP) - 244 901

Email: sanjeev26876@gmail.com, *Mob.:* +91-9412309073

PRESENT SCENARIO

As per estimates, inadequate sanitation cost India almost $54 billion or 6.4% of the country's GDP in 2006. Over 70% of this economic impact or about $38.5 billion was health-related, with diarrhea followed by acute lower respiratory infections accounting for 12% of the health-related impacts. Evidence suggests that all water and sanitation improvements are cost-beneficial in all developing world sub-regions.

Sectoral demands for water are growing rapidly in India owing mainly to urbanization and it is estimated that by 2025, more than 50% of the country's population will live in cities and towns. Population increase, rising incomes, and industrial growth are also responsible for this dramatic shift. National Urban Sanitation Policy 2008 was the recent development in order to rapidly promote sanitation in urban areas of the country. India's Ministry of Urban Development commissioned the survey as part of its National Urban Sanitation Policy in November 2008. In rural areas, local government institutions in charge of operating and maintaining the infrastructure are seen as weak and lack the financial resources to carry out their functions. In addition, no major city in India is known to have a continuous water supply and an estimated 72% of Indians still lack access to improved sanitation facilities.

CONSTRUCTIVE STRATEGIES: A POSITIVE ASPECT

A number of innovative approaches to improve water supply and sanitation have been tested in India, in particular in the early 2000s. These include demand-driven approaches in rural water supply since 1999, community-led total sanitation, public–private partnerships to improve the continuity of urban water supply and the use of microcredit to women in order to improve access to water.

Total sanitation campaign gives strong emphasis on Information, Education, and Communication (IEC), capacity building and hygiene education for effective behavior change with involvement of panchayati raj institutions (PRIs), community-based organizations and nongovernmental organizations (NGOs), etc. The key intervention areas are individual household latrines (IHHL), school sanitation and hygiene education (SSHE), community sanitary complex, Anganwadi toilets supported by Rural Sanitary Marts (RSMs), and production centers (PCs). The main goal of the government of India (GOI) is to eradicate the practice of open defecation by 2010. To give fillip to this endeavor, GOI has launched Nirmal Gram Puraskar to recognize the efforts in terms of cash awards for fully covered PRIs and those individuals and institutions who have contributed significantly in ensuring full sanitation coverage in their area of operation. The project is being implemented in rural areas taking district as a unit of implementation.

A recent study highlighted that policy shift to include better household water quality management to complement the continuing expansion of coverage and upgrading of services would appear to be a cost-effective health intervention in many developing countries. Most of the interventions (including multiple interventions, hygiene, and water quality) were found to significantly reduce the levels of diarrheal illness, with the greatest impact being seen for hygiene and household treatment interventions. Interventions to improve water quality at the household level are more effective than those at the source. Unfortunately, in developing countries, public health concerns are usually raised on the institutional setting, such as municipal services, hospitals, and environmental sanitation. There is a reluctance to acknowledge the home as a setting of equal importance along with the public institutions in the chain of disease transmission in the community. Managers of home hygiene and community hygiene must act in unison to optimize return from efforts to promote public health.

The role of the WHO Guidelines for Drinking Water Quality emphasizes an integrated approach to water quality assessment and management from source to consumer. It emphasizes on quality protection and prevention of contamination and advises to be proactive and participatory, and address the needs of those in developing countries who have no access to piped community water supplies. The guidelines emphasize the maintenance of microbial quality to prevent waterborne infectious disease as an essential goal. In addition, they address protection from chemical toxicants and other contaminants of public health concern.

When sanitation conditions are poor, water quality improvements may have minimal impact regardless of amount of water contamination. If each transmission pathway alone is sufficient to maintain diarrheal disease, single-pathway interventions will have minimal benefit, and ultimately an intervention will be successful only if all sufficient pathways are eliminated. However, when one pathway is critical to maintaining the disease, public health efforts should focus on this critical pathway. The positive impact of improved water quality is greatest for families living under good sanitary conditions, with the effect statistically significant when sanitation is measured at the community level but not significant when sanitation is measured at the household level. Improving drinking water quality would have no effect in neighborhoods with very poor environmental sanitation; however, in areas with better community sanitation, reducing the concentration of fecal coliforms by two orders of magnitude would lead to a 40% reduction in diarrhea. Providing private excreta disposal would be expected to reduce diarrhea by 42%, while eliminating excreta around the house would lead to a 30% reduction in diarrhea. The findings suggest that improvements in both water supply and sanitation are necessary if infant health in developing countries is to be improved. They also imply that it is not epidemiologic but behavioral, institutional, and economic factors that should correctly determine the priority of interventions. Another study highlighted that water quality interventions to the point-of-use water treatment were found to be more effective than previously thought, and multiple interventions (consisting of combined water, sanitation, and hygiene measures) were not more effective than interventions with a single focus. Studies have shown that hand washing can reduce diarrhea episodes by about 30%. This significant reduction is comparable to the effect of providing clean water in low-income areas.

Lack of safe water supply, poor environmental sanitation, improper disposal of human excreta, and poor personal hygiene help to perpetuate and spread diarrheal diseases in India. Since diarrheal diseases are caused by 20–25 pathogens, vaccination, though an attractive disease prevention strategy, is not feasible. However, as the majority of childhood diarrheas are caused by *Vibrio cholerae, Shigellae dysenteriae* type 1, rotavirus, and enterotoxigenic Escherichia coli which have a high morbidity and mortality, vaccines against these organisms are essential for the control of epidemics. A strong political will with appropriate budgetary allocation is essential for the control of childhood diarrheal diseases in India.

National water policies are shifting to community-based management approach because local authorities are in daily contact with users, of whom about 50% are women. Historically, national policy shifted from attention to distribution of investments in the water sector to reorganization of water agencies and to building up the capacity of private or voluntary agencies. The local context allows for more efficient and effective responses to local conditions. Local institutions and groups are better equipped to solicit local participation. Local water resource planning is very important in strengthening the economic and individual capacity of poor people in underdeveloped areas.

Providing private excreta disposal would be expected to reduce diarrhea by 42%, while eliminating excreta around the house would lead to a 30% reduction in diarrhea. The findings suggest that improvements in both water supply and sanitation are necessary if infant health in developing countries is to be improved.

India still loses between 0.4 and 0.5 million children under 5 years due to diarrhea. While infant mortality and under 5 mortality rates have declined over the years for the country as a whole, in many states, these have stagnated in recent years. One of the reasons is the failure to make significant headway in improving personal and home hygiene, especially in the care of young children and the conditions surrounding birth.

The agriculture sector accounts for between 90 and 95% of surface and ground water in India, while industry and the domestic sector account for the remaining. At the same time, several important measures are being taken to deal with the above issues. On the water resources management front, the National Water Policy, 2002 recognizes the need for well-developed information systems at the national and state levels, places strong emphasis on nonconventional methods for utilization such as interbasin transfers, artificial recharge, desalination of brackish or sea water, as well as traditional water conservation practices such as rainwater harvesting, etc., to increase utilizable water resources. It also advocates watershed management through extensive soil conservation, catchment area treatment, preservation of forests, and increasing forest cover and the construction of check dams. The policy also recognizes the potential need to reorganize and reorient institutional arrangements for the sector and emphasizes the need to maintain existing infrastructure.

It is important to reiterate the need for Rural Water Supply and Sanitation [RWSS] and Urban Water Supply and Sanitation [UWSS] agencies to operate hand-in-hand with their health and education counterparts to jointly monitor indicators of RWSS, UWSS, health, education, poverty, and equity in order to make significant headway in the respective sectors. Existing health promotion and education programmes should be made more effective and geared toward achieving behavior changes needed to improve hygiene.

Percent of urban population without proper sanitation in India is 63%. The 11th five year plan envisages 100% coverage of urban water, urban sewerage, and rural sanitation by 2012. Although investment in water supply and sanitation is likely to see a jump of 221% in the 11th plan over the 10th plan, the targets do not take into account both the quality of water being provided, or the sustainability of systems being put in place. Increasing emphasis on use of information technology applications in urban governance and management to ensure quick access to information, planning, and decision support systems are the primary concern areas related to environmental sanitation. Solid waste management is also increasingly seen as an important area in UWSS. Legislation on municipal waste handling and management has been passed in October 2000. Some strategies on solid waste management include preparation of town-wise master plans, training of municipal staff, IEC and awareness generation, involvement of community-based and nongovernmental organizations, setting up and operation of compost plants via NGOs and the private sector, enhancement of the capacities of some state structures such as State Compost Development Corporations with emphasis on commercial operations and private sector involvement. Variations in housing type, density and settlement layout, poverty status, and access to networked services will lead to different solutions for sanitation in different parts of the city or within the same neighborhood.

CHALLENGES: HEALTH AND ENVIRNOMENTAL SANITATION

1. Prevention of contamination of water in distribution systems.
2. Growing water scarcity and the potential for water reuse and conservation.
3. Implementing innovative low-cost sanitation system.
4. Providing sustainable water supplies and sanitation for urban and semi-urban areas.
5. Reducing disparities within the regions in the country.
6. Sustainability of water and sanitation services.

POSSIBLE SOLUTIONS

Following are important prerequisites to be considered to bring the changes:

- Implementation of low-cost sanitation system with lower subsidies.
- Greater household involvement
- Range of technology choices
- Construction of sanitary complexes for women.
- Rural drainage systems,
- IEC and awareness building.

- Involvement of NGOs and local groups.
- Availability of finance
- Human resource development.
- Emphasis on school sanitation.
- Appropriate forms of private participation and public private partnerships.
- Evolution of a sound sector policy in Indian context
- Emphasis on sustainability with political commitment.

CONCLUSION

Drinking water supply and sanitation in India continue to be inadequate, despite longstanding efforts by the various levels of government and communities at improving coverage. The level of investment in water and sanitation, albeit low by international standards. A number of innovative approaches to improve water supply and sanitation have been tested in India. Most Indians depend on on-site sanitation facilities. The lack of adequate sanitation and safe water has significant negative health impacts. Depleting ground water table and deteriorating ground water quality are threatening the sustainability of both urban and rural water supply in many parts of India. The supply of cities that depend on surface water is threatened by pollution, increasing water scarcity and conflicts among users.

Although, clean water supply and sanitation is a Government responsibility, but individual efforts are necessary. In November 2008 the government of India launched a national urban sanitation policy with the goal of creating what it calls "totally sanitized cities" that are open-defecation free, safely collect and treat all their wastewater, eliminate manual scavenging and collect and dispose solid waste safely. Future of health and sanitation in India is full of new perspectives that resumes clean water service, especially to the poor, which is difficult to access and is provided at inconvenient hours of the day; fulfilling of industrial water needs; increased sanitary facilities that are too few in number and often unusable; and management of urban drains, creeks and coastal waters that are polluted with sanitary and industrial wastes.

REFERENCES

1. Ganesh S Kumar, Sitanshu Sekhar Kar, and Animesh Jain (2011) Health and Environmental Sanitation in India: Issues for Prioritizing Control Strategies. Indian J Occup Environ Med., 15(3): 93-96.

2. Asian Development Bank: 2007 Benchmarking and Data Book of Water Utilities in India, 2007, p. 3.
3. National Institute of Urban Affairs: Status of Water Supply, Sanitation and Solid Waste Management, 2005, p. xix-xxvi.
4. Gtz: Ecological Sanitation – A Need of Today! Progress of Ecosan in India, 2006, p. 3.
5. Planning Commission (India): Draft Report of the Steering Committee on Urban Development for Eleventh Five Year Plan (2007-2012), 2007. Retrieved 15 April 2010.
6. Joint Monitoring Programme for Water Supply and Sanitation Estimate for 2008 Based on the 2006 Demographic and Health Survey, the 2001 Census, Other Data and the Extrapolation of Previous Trends to 2010.
7. Planning Commission of India (2010) Health and Family Welfare and AYUSH : 11th Five Year Plan, p. 78.
8. National Institute of Urban Affairs: Status of Water Supply, Sanitation and Solid Waste Management, 2005, p. 28.
9. A Special Report on India: Creaking, Groaning: Infrastructure is India's Biggest Handicap". *The Economist*. 11 December 2008.
10. Planning Commission: India Water Supply and Sanitation Assessment 2002, a WHO-UNICEF Sponsored Study, 2003, p. 23-26.
11. Planning Commission of India: India Assessment 2002, Water Supply and Sanitation, a WHO-UNICEF Sponsored Study, 2003, p. 51-53.
12. OECD, 2007: Measuring Aid to Water Supply and Sanitation, p. 3.
13. GTZ: Sustainable Sanitation in India. Examples from Indo-German Development Cooperation, November 2008.
14. World Bank Water and Sanitation Programme (WSP): (September 2010). "The Karnataka Urban Water Sector Improvement Project: 24 x 7 Water Supply is Achievable" (PDF). Retrieved 20 August 2012.

Pages: 125-133

WASTE MANAGEMENT AND ENVIRONMENTAL HEALTH

Edited by: **Dr. B. Tabassum; Dr. Priya Bajaj & Dr. Pawan Kumar 'Bharti'**

ISBN: 978-93-5056-777-7

Edition: **2016**

Published by: **Discovery Publishing House Pvt. Ltd., New Delhi (India)**

Bioremediation of Textile Waste Effluents by *Chlorella Vulgaris*

Alina Javed

ABSTRACT

The microalgae biomass production from textile waste effluent is a possible solution for the environmental impact generated by the effluent discharge into water sources. The potential application of *Chlorella vulgaris* for bioremediation of textile waste effluent (WE) was investigated using 2^2 Central Composite Design (CCD). This work addresses the adaptation of the microalgae *C. vulgaris* in textile waste effluent (WE) and the study of the best dilution of the WE for maximum biomass production and for the removal of colour and Chemical Oxygen Demand (COD) by this microalgae. The cultivation of C. vulgaris, presented

Department of Biotechnology, Jamia Millia Islamia, New Delhi.

Email: alina.ally1@gmail.com

Corresponding Author: Alina Javed, Azad Colony, Infront of Ahteram Medical Store, Saharanpur (UP)

E-mail: alina.ally1@gmail.com, *Mob.:* +917417699239

maximum cellular concentrations C_{max} and maximum specific growth rates I_{max} in the wastewater concentration of 5.0% and 17.5%, respectively. The highest colour and COD removals occurred with 17.5% of textile waste effluent. The results of *C. vulgaris* culture in the textile waste effluent demonstrated the possibility of using this microalgae for the colour and COD removal and for biomass production. There was a significant negative relationship between textile waste effluent concentration and C_{max} at 0.05 level of significance. However, sodium bicarbonate concentration did not significantly influence the responses of C_{max} and the removal of colour and COD.

Keywords: *C. Vulgaris,* Bioremediation, Textile wastes & Microalgae

INTRODUCTION

Synthetic dye usage has increased in the textile and dyeing industries because of their ease and cost-effectiveness in synthesis, firmness, high stability to light, temperature, detergent and microbial attack and variety in colour compared with natural dyes. The major environmental problem associated with the use of dyes is their lose during dyeing process since the fixation efficiency ranges from 60 to 90%.

The release of coloured wastewaters in the ecosystem is a dramatic source of esthetic pollution, eutrophication, and perturbations including decrease in the photosynthetic activity and dissolved oxygen (DO) as well as alteration of the pH, increase in the biochemical oxygen demand (BOD) and chemical oxygen demand (COD), in aquatic life. Therefore, treatment of these industrial effluents is necessary prior to their final discharge to the environment. Various physical/chemical methods have been used for the removal of dyes from wastewaters. These methods have some drawbacks, such as not all dyes, currently used can be degraded or removed with physical and chemical processes and sometimes the degradation products are more toxic. So that treatment methods must be tailored to the chemistry of the dyes. Microbial and enzymatic decolorization and degradation of azo dyes have significant potential to address this problem due to their environmentally-friendly, inexpensive nature, and also they do not produce large quantities of sludge.

METHODS

- Textile effluent can be characterized by collecting it from the region of waste discharge.
- Store it under cooling to 4 °C.

- Samples are immediately fixed with 4% formaldehyde for laboratory analysis and microalgae are counted and identified using 2 ml settling chambers with a Nikon TS 100 inverted microscope at 400x magnification.
- The dominant algal strain, *Chlorella vulgaris* is used throughout the study work.
- The alga strain *C. vulgaris* is isolated and purified in axenic cultures and used throughout this study.
- A 2^2 Central Composite Design (CCD) is used to study the influence of the wastewater concentration and sodium bicarbonate concentration on the *C. vulgaris* growth and the removal of wastewater pollutants.

RESULT

Table 12.1: Physicochemical Characteristics of the Textile Industrial Effluent WE

Sl. No.	Parameter	Unit	Value
1.	Colour intensity	Absorbance at 660nm	0.114
2.	pH	–	8.05
3.	Conductivity	mS	10.23
4.	TS	mgl^{-1}	735
5.	TDS	mgl^{-1}	506
6.	COD	mgO_2l^{-1}	51.2
7.	P	$\mu g\ l^{-1}$	0.96
8.	NO_2	$\mu g\ l^{-1}$	0.55
9.	NO_3	$\mu g\ l^{-1}$	1.95
10.	Ca	$mg\ l^{-1}$	140.28
11.	Mg	$mg\ l^{-1}$	159.72

Table 12.2: Heavy Metals Present in Textile Industrial Effluent WE

Sl. No.	Heavy Metal	Amount ($mg\ l^{-1}$)
1.	Cu	7.05
2.	Zn	8.61
3.	Cr	6.33
4.	Mn	10.5
5.	Fe	380.4

Microalgae Flora Present in the WE

Algal flora that occurred in the WE were identified. The results revealed that the species belonging to 4 families were identified. The mean total phytoplankton cell abundance was 353, 552, 4 cells l^{-1}. The temporal pattern showed the presence of 26 taxons recorded that Chlorophyta made up the highest number (44.65%) and are represented by (8 genera, 14 species). *Chlorella vulgaris* is the most dominant species of Chlorophyta.

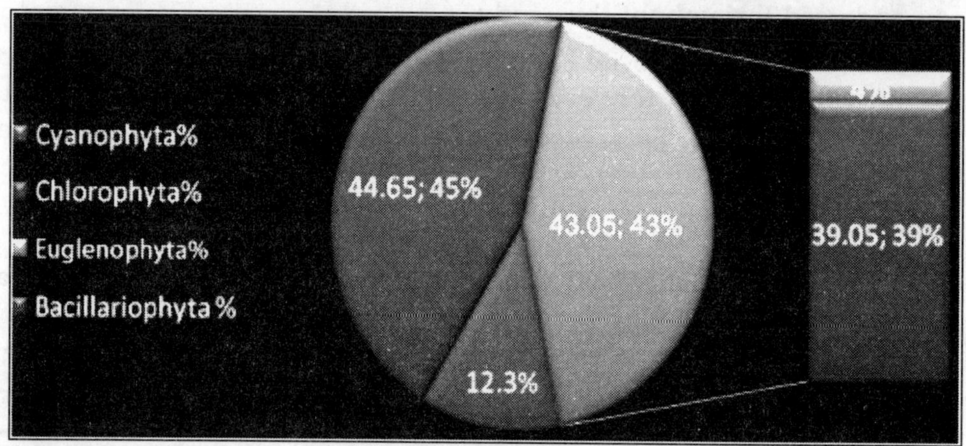

Fig. 12.1: **Percentage Abundance of the Microalgae Groups in the WE**

Cultivation of the Microalgae *C. vulgaris* and Pollutants Removal Alga Growth

The results presented graphically show the growth curves of *C. Vulgaris* obtained for each run of factorial design. The results represent the maximum specific growth rate ($\grave{\imath}_{max}$) and C_{max} of the 1st to 10th runs of the factorial design for evaluating the influence of the concentrations of both wastewater and sodium bicarbonate on the growth of the microalga *C. vulgaris*, as well as the reduction of colour and COD. The largest SBC in 3rd run (13.5%), compared to 1st run (6.5%), caused no increasing of the values of $\grave{\imath}_{max}$ and C_{max}. The 5th run, which was accomplished with the smallest WC (5.0%), SBC of 10.0 g l^{-1}, obtained the largest C_{max} of 270,009 cells ml^{-1}.

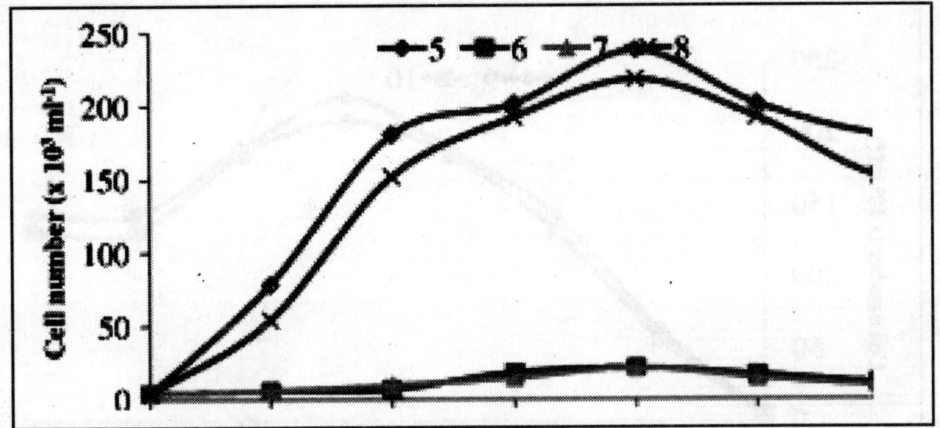

Fig. 12.2: **Time Course of *C. vulgaris* Cell Numbers (cells ml^{-1}) for 1-4 Runs of the CCD**
1st run (WC = 8.5%; SBC = 6.5 g l^{-1});
2nd run (WC = 26.5%; SBC = 6.5 g l^{-1});
3rd run (WC = 8.5%; SBC = 13.5 g l^{-1})
4th run (WC = 26.5%; SBC = 13.5 g l^{-1}).
(WC: Wastewater Concentration; SBC: Sodium Bicarbonate Concentration)

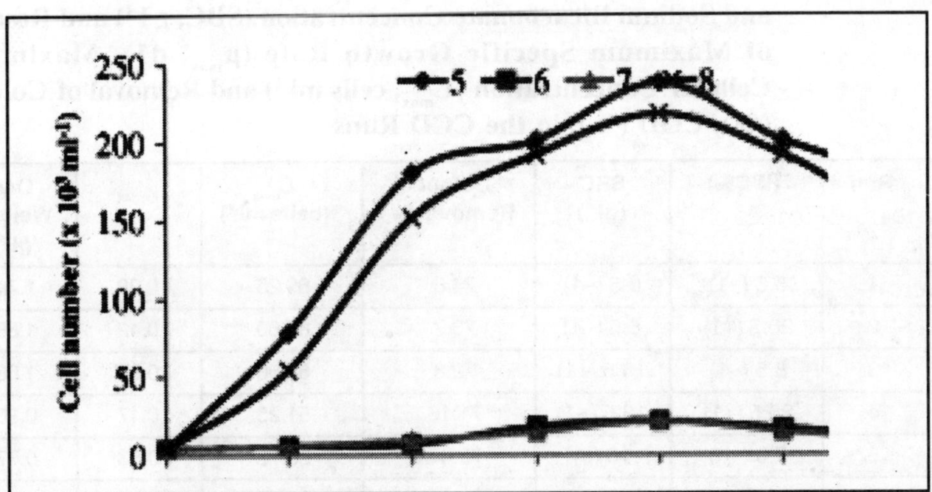

Fig. 12.3: **Time Course of *C. vulgaris* Cell Numbers (cells ml^{-1}) for 5-8 Runs of the CCD**
5th run (WC = 5.0%; SBC = 10.0 g l^{-1});
6th run (WC = 30.0%; SBC = 10.0 g l^{-1});
7th (WC = 17.5%; SBC = 5.0 g l^{-1})
8th run (WC = 17.5%; SBC = 15.0 g l^{-1}).
(WC: Wastewater Concentration; SBC: Sodium Bicarbonate Concentration)

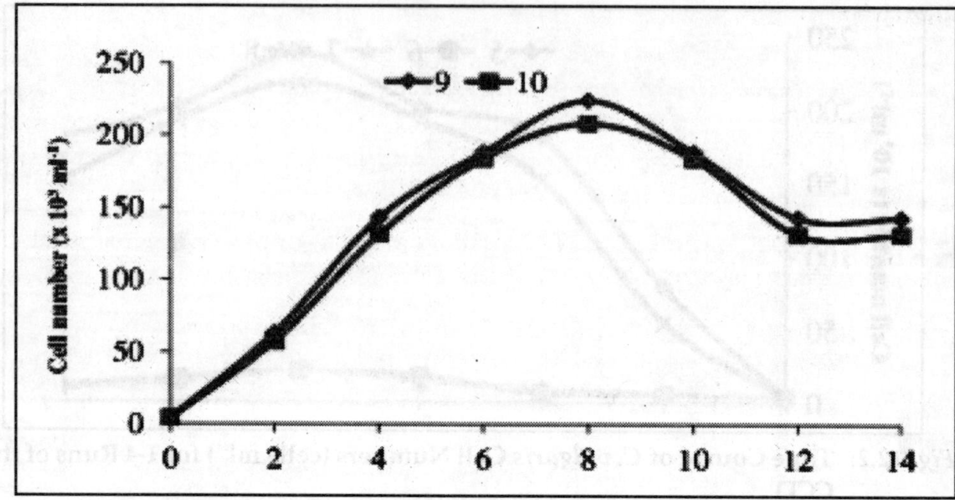

Fig. 12.4: Time Course of *C. vulgaris* Cell Numbers (cells ml^{-1}) for 9th and 10th Runs of CCD
9th run (WC = 17.5%; SBC = 10.0 g l^{-1})
10th run (WC = 17.5%; SBC = 10.0 g l^{-1}).
(WC: Wastewater Concentration; SBC: Sodium Bicarbonate Concentration)

Table 12.3: Coded and Real Values of Wastewater Concentration (WC%) and Sodium Bicarbonate Concentration (SBC, g l^{-1}) and Results of Maximum Specific Growth Rate (μ_{max}, d1), Maximum Cellular Concentration (C_{max}, cells ml^{-1}) and Removal of Colour (%), COD (%), in the CCD Runs

Run	(WC%)	SBC (gl^{-1})	Colour Removal %	C_{max} (cells ml^{-1})	μ_{max}	Dry Weight (gl^{-1})
1.	8.5 (–1)	6.5 (–1)	74.6	69.25	0.89	1.74
2.	26.5 (+1)	6.5 (–1)	73.7	65.60	0.42	1.88
3.	8.5 (–1)	13.5 (+1)	72.8	67.50	0.87	1.68
4.	26.5 (+1)	13.5 (+1)	71.16	51.25	0.47	0.90
5.	5.0 (–α)	10 (0)	72.07	53.75	0.53	0.77
6.	30.0 (+α)	10 (0)	74.66	63.13	0.56	0.88
7.	17.5 (0)	5 (–α)	71.28	63.50	0.26	0.86
8.	17.5 (0)	15 (+α)	76.32	49.10	0.53	1.55
9.	17.5 (0)	10 (0)	75.40	63.75	0.52	1.50
10.	17.5 (0)	10 (0)	75.68	69.90	0.52	1.49

DISCUSSION

Some scientists studied the cultivation of *C. vulgaris,* from textile waste effluent; they stated that the dilution of the textile waste effluents is an important factor affecting the algal growth and biomass productivity. Moreover *C. vulgaris* grew in 100% waste effluent; although the final biomass attained was significantly lower ($p < 0.05$) than that grown in 20–80% textile waste concentration. However, some people reported that *C. vulgaris* UMACC 001 was shown to be a versatile alga that is able to grow under various harsh conditions.

In this study *C. vulgaris* succeeded in decolorizing the WE during all the studied runs. It has been reported that several species of *Chlorella* are capable of degrading azo dyes to their aromatic amines and further metabolize the aromatic amines to simpler organic compounds or CO_2 and thereby detoxifying them. *C. vulgaris* decolorizes a variety of azo dyes via algal azo-dye reductase enzyme.

It has been suggested that the dye removal may be attributed to the accumulation of dye ions on the surface of algal biopolymers and further to the diffusion of the dye molecules from aqueous phase onto solid phase of the biopolymer. It has also been stated that colour removal by algae was due to three intrinsically different mechanisms of assimilative utilization of chromophores for the production of algal biomass, CO_2 and H_2O transformation of coloured molecules to non-coloured molecules, and adsorption of chromophores on algal biomass.

The final COD concentrations recorded at the end of all runs were smaller than the control value, confirming the COD removal during the time of this research study. This can be explained by the fact that Photosynthetic organisms and microalgae produce oxygen that enhances the biological degradation of the organic matter in the wastewaters. COD removal might not have been accomplished exclusively by *C. vulgaris;* but also by other factors including the chemical oxidation caused by the aeration of the culture as well as microorganisms in the wastewater, which can promote the COD reduction of the medium.

The phytoremediation of the textile industrial WE may be accomplished by phosphorous removal which could have started by two different mechanisms: by the biological assimilation during the biomass growth and by the chemical precipitation that occurred predominantly when the biomass concentration decreases, as during the decline phase or cellular death.

The waste grown algal biomass may not be suitable for use as animal feed. However, there has been increased interest in using algae for biodiesel production. The treatment system employing this algal design will be useful to decolorize and detoxify the textile industrial WE before discharge and algal biomass can be analyzed for lipid contents for further use in biofuel production.

CONCLUSIONS AND FUTURE DIRECTIONS

The microalgae *C. vulgaris,* grown on the we showed C_{max} (270,009 cells ml^{-1}), μ_{max} (0.53 d^{-1}) in the smaller wastewater concentration added to the cultivation medium (5.0 and 8.5%), while larger COD removals (69.25 and 69.90%) and the largest colour removals (75.68%) were obtained using the moderate waste water concentration in the cultivation medium. Thus the cultivation of *C. vulgaris* in WE demonstrated the capability of biomass production, colour and COD removal; therefore this microalga can be an alternative to assist in the textile culture effluent treatment, reducing the environmental impact caused by their pollutants. The algal biomass generated may be useful as feedstock, fertilizers or for biofuel production.

REFERENCES

1. Abadulla *et al.*, 2000 E. Abadulla, T. Tzanov, S. Costa, K.H. Robra, A. Cavaco-Paulo, *etal.* Decolorization and Detoxification of Textile Dyes with a Laccase from *Trametes hirsute.* Appl. Environ. Microbiol., 66 (2000), pp. 3357-3362.

2. Acuner and Dilek, 2004. E. Acuner, F.B. Dilek. Treatment of Tectilon Yellow 2G by *Chlorella vulgaris.* Proc. Biochem., 3(2004), pp. 623-631.

3. Amin *et al.*, 2008. H. Amin, A. Amer, A. El Fecky, I. Ibrahim. Treatment of Textile Waste Water Using H_2O_2/UV System. Physicochem. Probl. Miner. Process., 42 (2008), pp. 17-28.

4. APHA, 2000. APHA American Public Health Association. Standard Methods for Examination of Water and Wastewater (21st ed.)Washington, DC, USA (2000)

5. Aslan and Kapdan, 2006. S. Aslan, I.K. Kapdan. Batch Kinetics of Nitrogen and Phosphorus Removal from Synthetic Wastewater by Algae. Ecol. Eng., 28 (1) (2006), pp. 64-70.

6. Brito *et al.*, 2007. A. Brito, J. Peixoto, J. Oliveira, J. Oliveira, C. Costa, R. Nogueira, A. Rodrigues. Brewery and Winery Wastewater Treatment: Some Focal Points of Design and Operation. V. Oreopoulou, W. Russ (Eds.), Utilization of By-Products and Treatment of Waste in the Food Industry, Springer, ISEKI-Food (2007), pp. 109-131.

7. Couto, 2009. S.R. Couto. Dye Removal by Immobilized Fungi. Biotechnol. Adv., 27 (2009), pp. 227-235.

8. Daneshvar *et al.*, 2007. N. Daneshvar, M. Ayazloo, A.R. Khataee, M. Pourhassan. Biological Decolorization of Dye Solution Containing Malachite Green by Microalgae *Cosmarium*sp. Bioresour. Technol., 98 (2007), p. 1176.

9. dos Santos *et al.*, 2007. A.B. dos Santos, F.J. Cervantes, J.B. Van Lier. Review Paper on Current Technologies for Decolorization of Textile Waste Water: Perspective for Anaerobic Biotechnology. Bioresour. Technol., 98 (2007), pp. 2369-2385.

10. El-Sheekh *et al.*, 2009. M.M. El-Sheekh, M.M. Gharieb, G.W. Abou-El-Souod. Biodegradation of Dyes by Some Green Algae and Cyanobacteria. Int. Biodeterior. Biodegrad., 63 (2009), pp. 699-704.

11. Gupta *et al.*, 2006. V.K. Gupta, A. Rastogi, V.K. Saini, N. Jain. Biosorption of Copper (II) from Aqueous Solutions by *Spirogyra* species. J. Colloid Interface Sci., 296 (2006), pp. 59-63.

Index